AF797885

Writing for Clarity

U. S. Probation/Pretrial Edition

Danny Kuhn

with

Hilarie Gaylin

Writing for Clarity

U. S. Probation/Pretrial Edition

Published by Favoritetrainers.com Books

763 Murray Avenue, Myrtle Beach SC 29577

www.favoritetrainers.com

Copyright © 2017 Danny R. Kuhn

All rights reserved. No portion of this book may be reproduced in any form without permission from the publisher, except as permitted by U. S. copyright law.

Cover and Illustrations by Seth Ellison

ISBN: 0-9891696-7-7
ISBN-13: 978-0-9891696-7-7

DEDICATION

This work is dedicated to the staff at the Court Education Division of the Federal Judicial Center, Washington, D.C. They are outstanding civil servants, outstanding trainers, and outstanding friends.

CONTENTS

ACKNOWLEDGMENTS

Thanks to:

-Hilarie Gaylin, without whose professional editing this book would be of little use.

-Jim Patterson and Eddie Samson, my training partners, who remind me how silly I sound each year when I say I am going to give up on-site training to just write books, walk the dog, and run the vacuum cleaner.

-Angela Long, Phyllis Drum, Joy Richardson, Jim Buchannan, Mark Sherman, Lori Murphy, Jane Goldman Nelson, Michael Siegel, and the rest of the staff at the Federal Judicial Center Court Education Division, as well as past staff members Nancy Filsoof, Kate Lynott, Bob Luke, Marilyn Vernon, and Barbara Anderson. They are all dedicated, talented, and conscientious people who have been as much family as work colleagues over the years.

-Seth Ellison, for his perfectly on-point cartoons.

SALT
Pepper
Commas

1 PREFACE/COMMA SENSE IS AN UNCOMMON VIRTUE

Before we take on the most contentious grammar issue of them all, a few words about *Writing for Clarity:*

During my 20-year career as a United States Probation Officer, I performed all our functions: Presentences, Pretrial, and Supervision. I also served as one of the Federal Judicial Center's volunteer field trainers for numerous programs across the country.

My final nine years in service were spent as DCUSPO for the Southern District of West Virginia. Since we were a relatively small district, several line officers fell under my direct supervision, and I spent part of most days proofing reports to the court. It seemed I corrected the same mistakes again and again, so I started keeping track of them, and at the end of six months, designed a simple training program for my own staff, hoping to spend less time proofing and correcting as a result. I thought that would be the end of it.

It wasn't. I did the three-hour class as a "we have some time to fill" presentation at a 4th Circuit Probation/Pretrial conference a few months later.

That was in 2005, and the requests for the class have continued, even after my 2010 retirement. I have presented the class from New Hampshire to Guam. Participants seem appreciative that the content has been written specifically for them, with references and examples directly from their work.

The most gratifying thing about presenting the program is the attitude change I often see from the beginning to the end. At the beginning, participants look like they just came to a writing class. *Glum.*

I get that. Given our past experiences and with so many other necessary things to do, not many United States Probation staff members are likely to have awakened that morning thinking, "Finally! Today is the day of the WRITING CLASS!" Instead, they file in hoping there will at least be coffee and pastries, people's expressions looking like they have just chewed aspirin. That's why I worked just as hard to make the class entertaining and immediately relevant as I did to research the grammar and style. Almost each class, I get what I consider the greatest compliment one can get for a writing class.

"Gee, this wasn't nearly as boring as I thought it would be!"

I'll take it.

I enjoy traveling to present "Writing for Clarity" and my other federal court classes, but several people suggested that I produce a small manual for ready USPO/USPTSO reference. This is that manual, and I hope you find it useful, though nothing can really replace live, interactive training.

WRITING AND GRAMMAR ARE NOT BLACK AND WHITE

You will find things here with which you disagree, and that's okay. Look at it this way: We refer to the United States Code and the Unites States Sentencing Guidelines almost every day. Those are law, cut-and-dried, and beyond dispute. They say what they say and that's that, right?

Of course not. If that were the case, most of us in the legal system would be out of jobs. There are inconsistencies, unanswered questions, and ambiguities. That's why we have courts.

Writing is much the same way. With the Code and Sentencing Guidelines, it's important to have the correct manual edition, right? What if there were several editions in the same year, released all at once, and each of which stated something slightly different? That's the case with writing. No matter how many current, prestigious style manuals one uses, the quest for absolute consistency will fail. Take a close look at the model presentence reports in the monograph, and you will find many subtle differences.

Those differences have led to some amusing encounters on the road. The *Writing for Clarity* class is sometimes presented at off-site retreats, but more often in the Probation or Pretrial Office training room. On several occasions, participants have scuttled to their offices during breaks, returned with a style manual, flopped it open in front of me, and pointed at an entry. "See here! NO COMMA! I told you so!"

That's not surprising. Our writing is personal to us, and we take it seriously. It's something we create. It comes directly from us and did not exist before we gave it life. In that way, it's like our children.

I have always tried to remember that, and so should you. *If you tell people their writing is bad, it's like saying they have an ugly baby.* In other words, be careful about how you criticize and correct writing, and recognize that your way may not always be the only way.

It's also funny how writing evokes such nostalgia. In each class, I hear stories of excellent high school teachers who made such strong impressions that, decades later, students still say, "But Mrs. Mott always said it was impolite to use the first person that way!" Mrs. Mott still looms large, and most of us have such a teacher in our past.

Don't fight it. Decide on one of the major style manuals, and stick with it. The differences will usually not be significant. For this work, I have mainly relied on *The Elements of Style* by Strunk and White, *The Gregg Reference Manual: A Manual of Style, Grammar, Usage, and Formatting* by William A. Sabin, and *The Chicago Manual of Style* from The University of Chicago Press. You are probably already familiar with one or more of these style guides from your college days. The first is a small, elegant little book that will fit in your pocket, while the others are bicep-building tomes. I will discuss them a bit more later.

Here's your warning that I use a very informal style for the explanation and commentary portions of this work, because it is designed to simulate my live classes, with a conversational tone and the occasional Probation Office anecdote for context.

That *is* what we do, after all.

While *Writing for Clarity* will be a useful reference (I hope), it is also a self-study course with many exercises, including extensive rewriting, punctuation, word choice, and others. Some of the rewriting exercises do not include "after" examples, because, when it comes to style and word choice rather than grammar technicalities, there is no one correct answer. Please find a study partner willing to complete these exercises and swap your work to critique and discuss.

GETTING STARTED WITH YOU-KNOW-WHAT

You probably guessed which topic we would tackle first. It is by far the most controversial. I have reasonable, well-educated, otherwise amiable people almost come to blows over comma placement.

Let's begin with an exercise. I know you won't look ahead for answers, since that would be a blatant breech of one of the Canons of the Code of Conduct. I think it's Number 47.

Instructions: Punctuate each of the following sentences as needed. Some may not need additional punctuation.

It's Just Comma Sense

1. The section number of the amendment has not been decided and the effective date has not been set.

2. The class helps officers overcome the obstacles of offender resistance resentment and skepticism.

3. The District adopted an innovative aggressive testing policy.

4. The Association directory which gets larger every year has more than 2,000 listings.

4a. The Association directory that was published in 2024 has more than 2,000 listings.

5. Beth Altman former USSC commissioner will be the keynote speaker.

5a. Former USSC Commissioner Beth Altman will be the keynote speaker.

6. Therefore the new position announcement will be delayed.

7. At best the presentence report will be ready by June 30.

8. If we fail to report significant violations we could lose our credibility with the Court.

9. I object shouted the AUSA responding to the public defender's question.

10. To miscalculate is human to mitigate divine.

11. I began going to the gym on October 1 2019 after being granted "fit time."

11a. I began going to the gym in October 2019 after being granted "fit time."

12. The test cups were piloted in Madison Wisconsin and other Midwestern offices.

13. Each time our confirmation tests go up a nickel it costs us $1000 over the fiscal year.

14. Mr. Stone would you be able to open the meeting while the Judge answers an important call?

15. That's significant improvement isn't it?

16. When the report is in the committee will vote on the amendment.

When I teach the class live, I usually ask participants to simply call out the number of commas they added to each sentence, and I let them know that I have a good feeling that they will all agree on the answers for the whole exercise. I add that, while no class has actually succeeded in agreeing so far, the record for coming closest to total agreement is held by the U. S. Probation Office in Las Cruces, New Mexico, and know the present class will, at least, beat that old milestone. And just what is that milestone? Let's find out.

It's Just Comma Sense *Answer Key*

1. The section number of the amendment has not been decided, and the effective date has not been set.

COMMAS: 1

RULE: Use a comma to separate the clauses of a compound sentence connected by a coordinating conjunction.

Of course, this is as far as the "everyone having the same answer" goes. I generally have zero, one, and two all represented. Don't feel bad. Those record holders in Las Cruces only got to sentence *number two* without disagreement.

The terms *compound sentence* and *coordinating conjunction* are the keys. A compound sentence is one with more than one subject and predicate. Both parts are perfectly good sentences that can stand alone. They can be called *independent clauses*, since they can stand independently of one another. The section number of the amendment has not been decided. The effective date has not been set.

Those are both great sentences. When you combine them into one sentence using a coordinating conjunction (a conjunction placed between words, phrases, clauses, or sentences of equal rank, e.g., **and, but, or, for, nor, so, and yet),** use a comma *before* the conjunction. Do not use a comma if there is only one independent clause.

The response to this explanation often gives me some information on the ages of the participants. If you know the words to "Conjunction Junction, What's Your Function?" most likely you are a Baby Boomer (like me) or Gen Xer.

2. The class helps officers overcome the obstacles of offender resistance, resentment, and skepticism.

COMMAS: 2

RULE: Use a comma to separate items in a series.

Many people would rather use only one comma in this sentence. Whether or not they know it, they stand in opposition to what is known as the Oxford Comma, defined as a comma used after the penultimate (last but one in a series of things; second to the last) item in a list of three or more items, before *and* or *or*. The Oxford Comma is most commonly known by its very academic British name, but, to be fair to our side of the pond, the oft-omitted punctuation mark is sometimes known as the Harvard Comma, or simply the serial comma.

Think about it. Without the second comma, resentment and skepticism seem to be coupled, somehow separate from resistance.

This is more just an academic eye-roll, especially, perhaps, in federal court. Just look at O'Connor v. Oakhurst Dairy, No. 16-1901 (1st Cir. 2017), decided by United States Court of Appeals Judges Lynch, Lipez, and Barron, appealed from the United States District Court, District of Maine, Honorable Nancy Torresen, Chief U. S. District Judge.

According to Maine state law, the following types of activities do not qualify for overtime pay:

The canning, processing, preserving, freezing, drying, marketing, storing, packing for shipment or distribution of:

(1) Agricultural produce;
(2) Meat and fish products; and
(3) Perishable foods.

There, in the comma-less space between the words "shipment" and "or," the case of *Kevin O'Connor v. Oakhurst Dairy* was argued. Is packing (for shipment or distribution) a single activity that is exempt from overtime pay? Or are packing and distributing two different activities, and both exempt?

If lawmakers had used an Oxford comma, it would have been clear that distribution was an overtime-exempt activity on its own. Without the comma (wrote US Court of Appeals Judge David J. Barron) the law is ambiguous as to whether distribution is a separate activity, or whether the whole last clause *packing for shipment or distribution* is one activity, meaning only the people who pack the dairy products are exempt. The drivers, Mr. Kevin O'Connor among them, do distribute, but do not pack, the perishable food. Mr. O'Connor believed he was entitled to overtime; the management of Oakhurst Dairy did not.

The District Court ruled in the company's favor, and O'Connor appealed. Arguments cited many style books, but the necessity of the Oxford Comma won the day, and O'Connor's case was sent back to District Court.

Think how unsettled the world would have been had I been awarded a plaque at a fancy Vatican ceremony back in the 1990s, and, in my acceptance speech, said, "I would like to thank my parents, Mother Teresa and the Pope."

What a headline in the *National Inquirer* that would have caused!

3. The District adopted an innovative, aggressive testing policy.

COMMAS: 1

RULE: Use a comma to separate two or more adjectives modifying the same noun if *and* could be used between them.

In this case, the comma simply takes the place of the word *and*. 'Innovative *and* aggressive' is also perfectly acceptable, but the comma makes the sentence a bit more concise.

4. The Association directory, which gets larger every year, has more than 2,000 listings.

COMMAS: 2

RULE: Use a comma to set off a nonrestrictive clause or phrase (one that if eliminated would not affect the meaning of the sentence).

Read the sentence again, leaving out *which gets larger every year.* The meaning of the sentence is unchanged. Sure, you have a bit more information, but the meaning is unambiguous.

4a. The Association directory that was published in 2024 has more than 2,000 listings.

COMMAS: 0

RULE: Commas should not be used when the clause is restrictive (essential to the meaning of the sentence):

Think back to the U. S. Code or Sentencing Guidelines. Remember that rule about the edition in effect at the time of the crime being used throughout the sentencing process, even if the law or guidelines changed? That scenario applies. The sentence refers to a specific directory version, the one published in 2024 as opposed to 2023 or 2025, and that makes the information essential to the meaning of the sentence.

5. Beth Altman, former USSC commissioner, will be the keynote speaker.

COMMAS: 2

RULE: Use a comma to set off words and phrases that are in apposition to (that are equivalent to) a noun or noun phrase.

This is one example of why English is such a tough language to study. Apposition? The closest word in sound is opposition, which means as far away as you can get from being the same as something else. Yet, apposition means *the same*. It means equal. Equivalent to. Beth Altman? Former USSC commissioner? They are equivalent and set off by commas.

5a. Former USSC Commissioner Beth Altman will be the keynote speaker.

COMMAS: 0

RULE: A comma should not be used if such words or phrases precede (come before) the noun they modify.

Who would think the order in which words come in a sentence makes that significant a difference? But it does. Go figure. By the way, you will notice commissioner is capitalized when it is placed before the person's name, but not when it comes after.

6. Therefore, the new position announcement will be delayed.

COMMAS: 1

RULE: Use a comma to set off transitional words and short expressions that require a pause in reading or speaking.

This is a rule that, like the law, opens room for disagreement in interpretation. I have known people who never require a pause in speaking until they turn blue in the face and collapse. I am not a fan of beginning sentences with transitional words like *therefore* in the first place. We will later discuss one of the legal system's very favorite opening words: *however*.

7. At best, the presentence report will be ready by June 30.

COMMAS: 1

Rule: Use a comma to set off words used to introduce a sentence if needed for clarity:

Again, "if needed" can be subjective. But clearly, the rule applies here. I can imagine the shakiness in the voice of a presentence writer giving this answer when a judge asks if a report can be completed early.

8. If we fail to report significant violations, we could lose our credibility with the Court.

COMMAS: 1

RULE: Use a comma to set off a subordinate clause or a long phrase that precedes a principle clause.

In Example 1, we mentioned independent clauses. "If we fail to report significant violations" is a *dependent clause.* It has several words and conveys quite a bit of information, but it does not have a subject and a predicate, so it does not meet the standard of being a complete sentence. The phrase is dependent on the rest of the words, the independent clause, to complete a thought. If dependent clauses come first in the sentence, use a comma.

9. "I object," shouted the AUSA, responding to the public defender's question.

COMMAS: 2, plus 2 quotation marks.

RULE: Use a comma to set off short quotations and sayings.

The main lesson here is the placement of the comma in relation to the quotation marks. It goes inside. Periods and exclamation marks also go inside quotation marks, unless you are writing by British standards.

10. To miscalculate is human; to mitigate, divine.

COMMAS: 1, plus 1 semicolon.

RULE: Use a comma to indicate omission of a word or words.

Tricky? This is the old adage "To err is human; to forgive, divine" written from the perspective of a presentence report writer. The original adage is often attributed to Alexander Pope and is written with broad poetic license.

In this case, the comma simply allows you to leave out the word *it,* with the proper pause. Why a semicolon instead of a comma? Two independent clauses are not joined by a comma; a semicolon must be used instead. To miscalculate is human. To mitigate (is) divine. Joining them together takes more than a comma, but only with the understood *it* in the second sentence, making it an independent clause. This is where participants remind me I have not yet covered semicolons and bemoan the unfairness of it all.

11. I began going to the gym on October 1, 2019, after being granted "fit time."

COMMAS: 2

RULE: Use a comma to set off the year from the month in full dates.

Leaving out the second comma is a common mistake.

11a. I began going to the gym in October 2019 after being granted "fit time."

COMMAS: 0

RULE: Omit the comma when only the month and the year are used.

After reading Example 11, you may find this example counterintuitive. The sentence loses only one element, the numerical date within October, but loses two commas.

12. The test cups were piloted in Madison, Wisconsin, and other Midwestern offices.

COMMAS: 2

RULE: Use a comma to set off city and state in geographic names.

Just like full dates, locations often incorrectly lose their second comma.

13. Each time our confirmation tests go up a nickel, it costs us $1,000 over the fiscal year.

COMMAS: 2

RULE: Use a comma to separate series of four or more figures into thousands, millions, and so on.

Tricky again? I'm sure you got the comma after 'nickel' because of Example 8, but did you put the comma in $1,000? In doing reports, you may find that it is often much easier to leave these commas out, especially when showing a column of numbers in a financial section. Numbers would line up so much better without those pesky little marks! But they are necessary.

14. Mr. Stone, would you be able to open the meeting while Judge Farber answers an important call?

COMMAS: 1

RULE: Use a comma to set off words used in direct address.

Direct address is stating the name or title of the person to whom you are speaking in the sentence. A pause is natural here when speaking to make sure you have the attention of the right person, and that's reflected in grammar as well.

15. That's significant improvement, isn't it?

COMMAS: 1

RULE: Use a comma to separate a question from the rest of the sentence.

Is the sentence a statement? Yes. Is it a question? Yes. When you have both elements in the same sentence, separate them with a comma.

16. When the report is in, the committee will vote on the amendment.

COMMAS: 1

RULE: Use a comma to set off any sentence elements that might be misunderstood if the comma were not used.

This is another rule that invites subjectivity, but the example shows its use clearly. Sometimes reports are *in committee*, (describing their location) so the speaker could, without the pause, give the wrong impression. Instead, we are waiting for the report to simply be *in*. Plus, in this example, the sentence begins with a dependent clause, removing the subjectivity.

Whew! So, the toughest part is behind you, right? Not quite. Commas are so important and are the source of so much disagreement that we will address them again with another exercise (and restated rules, to address differences in learning styles) later in this book.

In the meantime, it's time to stop using what appear to be the universal TWO SIMPLIFIED COMMA RULES:

1. When in doubt, leave one out.

2. Now and then, put one in.

Reading court documents, it's almost like we actually use these. Inserted a lot of commas? Stop for a while. Not used one in several sentences? Hand me the comma shaker and let me sprinkle in a few! We have seen grey areas in rule application, but just like with the law, there are actual rules to be followed. Practice will make their use more intuitive.

SEMICOLONS: NOT "SORT-OF COMMAS"

Using commas and semi-colons interchangeably is a common mistake. Some people seem to avoid semicolons altogether, even when only a semicolon will do.

Two of the most common semicolon uses in our type of writing are as follows:

1. To separate items in a list or series when any single element contains an internal comma or the enumeration follows a colon.

Example: The defendant has lived in Sweetwater, Texas; Paradise, Pennsylvania; Beauty, Kentucky, and Big Ugly, West Virginia.

NOT: The defendant has lived in Sweetwater, Texas, Paradise, Pennsylvania, Beauty, Kentucky, and Big Ugly, West Virginia.

Obviously, in the second sentence, there is no way to determine towns from states or in how many different places the defendant has lived.

And yes, all those place names are real. The first Chief Probation Officer for whom I worked carried a faded newspaper clipping in his wallet, a "society page" announcement:

CHARLESTON WOMAN TO WED BIG UGLY MAN

He used to pull it out to show almost everyone he met when we were together at conferences. After a while, people started avoiding him.

2. To unite two short, closely connected sentences.

The defendant returned the bottle. It had been filled with cocaine base.

Becomes The defendant returned the bottle; it had been filled with cocaine base.

The application can be made. No law states otherwise.

Becomes The application can be made; no law states otherwise.

Notice that the semicolon connects two complete sentences, making a single sentence constructed of two independent clauses. *A simple comma cannot do this without a conjunction.*

INCORRECT: The defendant returned the bottle, it had been filled with cocaine base.

ALSO INCORRECT: The application can be made, no law states otherwise.

Using a comma to join two independent clauses is known as a *comma splice*. The comma splice is everywhere. I mean *everywhere!* But that does not make it correct.

You definitely need a breather. More on commas later, with a different approach.

"Psssst... Did you recommend 5 years imprisonment or 5 years' imprisonment?"

2 THE GREENGROCER'S APOSTROPHE

Strange name, right? Only because we are on this side of the Atlantic. The term greengrocer is common in Great Britain. It's someone in the business of selling fruit and vegetables, or the business that person runs. In America, we may more commonly call this kind of business a produce stand, fruit stand, or farmer's market. In a large grocery store, we have the produce section, while our British friends have the greengrocery section. For some reason, the term just didn't make it over here.

Of course, the practice of grocery shopping has changed over the years. The large grocery store selling all types of food items under one roof (plus often things as decidedly non-edible as transmission fluid and disposable diapers) is primarily an American innovation that has now spread worldwide. While there are still holdout areas, Brits are no longer as likely to do daily food shopping at specialized shops, including the butcher, the fishmonger, the baker, and our friend the greengrocer.

When visiting small shops, stands, or yard sales, you can commonly see handmade signs telling you the cost of the items. While standardized signs in large chain retail establishments are more likely to be close to grammatically correct, small venues often exhibit the mistake of using an apostrophe to show a *plural* instead of a *possessive,* and that is the individual Greengrocer's Apostrophe.

If we are talking more generally about multiple vegetable sellers, I suppose it would be Greengrocers' Apostrophes.

Anyhow, it wouldn't surprise you to seek fresh "fruit and veg" and find handmade signs stating:

APPLE'S 69¢ lb

RUTABAGA'S 49¢ lb

NAVEL ORANGE'S 25¢ ea

So what? The court doesn't buy many fruits and vegetables. But, if you look carefully, you will find this mistake in places that surprise you, made by very educated writers who simply had a slip that was missed in proofreading. I have found the Greengrocer's Apostrophe in many court documents and at many other court venues. Not long ago, I taught at a conference that had helpful signs on the breakout session rooms:

OFFICER'S

CLERK'S

If the words *breakout room* been included on those signs, they would not be mentioned in this section, because OFFICER'S BREAKOUT ROOM is possessive, making the apostrophe necessary.

Some researchers date the term Greengrocer's Apostrophe to the mid-1900s, but I think it goes back further. I can imagine Dr. Samuel Johnson rising after an evening of stimulating conversation and brandy to browse the stalls of Portobello Road and smugly correcting the Cockney shopkeepers over EEL PIE'S - Tuppence.

Notice something about the paragraph above: *mid-1900s,* instead of the commonly-seen mid-*1900's.* What's possessive about it? A shrinking number of American style manuals allow the use of the apostrophe in referring to centuries, but most British manuals do not. The practice does become problematic with small numbers and single letters.

For example, "Dot the is and cross the ts" instead of "Dot the i's and cross the t's" obviously doesn't work. And during that mid-afternoon slump catching up on contacts, we can't blame you for visiting the vending machine for a bag of M&M's, apostrophe included.

I often receive Greengrocer's Apostrophe sign pictures taken by probation staff members who have attended my writing program. Once you start looking for the offending apostrophes, they pop out all over the place. Here are of memorable ones for me. I did *Writing for Clarity* for the ED/VA at Virginia Beach, and it was the final class before the conference ended at noon. I did not fly home until the following day, so I changed clothes and walked down the beach, following the sound of music and the smell of barbeque. I finally came to a gathering with a big sign proclaiming

WELCOME TO BLUE'S AT THE BEACH!

Did I mention I had *just* completed the *Writing for Clarity* class?

How could this sign be correct? If I had been walking into a pub named AT THE BEACH owned by a guy named BLUE, it would work. Otherwise, no.

Another one: The day after I retired from the United States Probation Office, I drove from West Virginia to Charleston, South Carolina, in order to visit with my old friend and former SD/WV colleague Ron Ward, the Director of the Probation and Pretrial Services Training Academy at FLETC. Having stowed my luggage at the Mills House, I walked down King Street until I found this sign:

HAPPY HOUR DRINK SPECIAL'S!

I knew I had found just the right spot to ease into private life after twenty years in federal service.

WHEN AN APOSTROPHE DOESN'T LOOK RIGHT, THINK TWICE.

To most of us now, especially after this exercise, the Greengrocer's Apostrophe just doesn't look right. It jumps out as being incorrect. But that tricky apostrophe also has a way of looking wrong when it is correct. For example, my forehead used to wrinkle at a sentence like this:

If convicted, the defendant faces a maximum sentence of five years' incarceration.

Not only is that writer using an unneeded apostrophe, he put it in the wrong place. Even the greengrocer wouldn't make that mistake, right?

But it isn't a mistake. To leave the apostrophe out, or to set it back a space, would be incorrect, no matter how "just not right" it looks. Here's how it works:

The incarceration of one year is a year's incarceration. (singular and possessive)

BUT: The incarceration of five years is five years' incarceration. (plural and possessive)

It's almost enough to make a proofreader give two weeks' notice!

Making a word that ends in *s* possessive also causes raised eyebrows and debate. The simple rule is to make a singular noun possessive by adding *'s*. Right?

Danny's book

The dog's bone

An offender's incarceration

Easy. But, what if the noun is singular *and already ends in s?* For example:

Charles, who has a firearm

Angus, who has bagpipes

A witness, who has evidence

Are you tempted to write Charles' son, Angus' bagpipes, witness' evidence? Many are. But the add *'s* rule is consistent regardless of the way the noun ends. Thus,

Charles's firearm

Angus's bagpipes

A witness's evidence

Some style guides will make an exception if the next word in the sentence also begins with *s*. In those cases, they suggest, the *s'* is preferred:

Charles' son

Angus' sword

A witness' statement

Some modernists even suggest going to the *s'* all the time, but I can't see any real justification to do so other than timidity. Some also lean toward using the way you would pronounce the word when speaking as the key to writing possessives. Charles's firearm is not pronounced the same as Charles' firearm.

Distributing **O**xycodone is a capital(ization) offense.

3 A CAPITAL(IZATION) OFFENSE

It's time for another exercise.

Instructions: The following drug names contain no capital letters. Circle any letters you would capitalize if you were using this drug name in the middle of a sentence.

oxycodone

penicillin

zocor

aspirin

acetaminophen

lorcet

oxycontin

hydrocodone

methadone

paxil

lipitor

metformin

glucophage

marijuana

antacid

codeine

cocaine

asmacort inhaler

theophylline

insulin

I'm sure you caught on immediately. If a drug name is a trademarked entity, the name is spelled exactly the way the trademark is registered. If the drug is an un-trademarked compound, it is not capitalized. But there are a few interesting wrinkles that sometimes make a simple rule hard to follow.

One, of course, is how do you know? As with so many other things, a simple Internet search will usually suffice. If the drug is trademarked, it will most likely have an official site sponsored by its manufacturer. WebMD, PDR.net, and the Physicians' Desk Reference are also good sources.

Here are the answers, with what could be a surprise or two:

oxycodone (not capitalized)

A single-ingredient opioid, one of many synthesized from the opium poppy.

penicillin (not capitalized)

Penicillin was the first successfully isolated and manufactured antibiotic. Many variations have been developed as bacteria became resistant over the years. Amoxicillin is an example, often known as the pink "bubble gum medicine" given to children for ear infections, etc. Penicillin is manufactured by many different pharmaceutical companies, under trademarked names, but if the medicine is generic, it is not capitalized. Many other, newer antibiotics are still prescribed in their non-generic, trademarked form. An example is azithromycin, marketed as Zithromax.

Zocor (capitalized)

The drug simvastatin is prescribed for high cholesterol and is manufactured with slight variations (commonly called statins) by several companies. One of the most common is Zocor, made by Merck.

aspirin (not capitalized *in the United States*)

Scientists from the German dye-making firm Bayer began marketing acetylsalicylic acid, originally extracted from willow bark, in 1899, and gave it the trademarked brand name Aspirin. But in a case fought out in our own federal courts, Bayer lost the trademark in 1918, affirmed by the appeals court in 1921. Thus, aspirin is a non-capitalized, non-trademarked generic term in the United States and many other countries. If you transfer to a probation office in Germany, though, be prepared to capitalize the word!

Believe it or not, heroin was also once a trademark of the Bayer Company. It lost the trademark in the Treaty of Versailles, the same treaty that ended World War I, in 1919. Since Bayer was a German company with a trademark and patent on what was at the time considered an effective pain reliever for war veterans, the victors took the spoils.

acetaminophen (not capitalized)

There are many, many cases in which the trademarked name of a newly-marketed substance becomes, in common speech, the substance's name, no matter which brand is at issue. I have never heard someone say, "I have a headache. Does anyone have acetaminophen?" Tylenol, of course, is a different matter, and as a registered brand of Johnson & Johnson Consumer Inc., is capitalized.

There are many instances of trademarked names becoming the generally accepted generic name, but that does not relieve us of the proper capitalization responsibility. Other examples? What would you capitalize in this sentence?

I used a *kleenex* and *q-tips* to wipe the *vaseline* off the *xerox* machine while drinking *coke* from my *thermos* and listening to my *walkman* but I cut my finger when I knocked over the *lava lamp* and needed a *band-aid.*

All nine items should be capitalized. Coke is a registered trademark of the Coca-Cola Company. Had the preceding word been *snorting* instead of *drinking*, heaven forbid, the word would not be capitalized.

Yes, I realize the use of *walkman* and *lava lamp* in the example dates me. I'm okay with that.

Lorcet (capitalized)

A combination drug made up of hydrocodone and acetaminophen, Lorcet is trademarked by Midlothian Laboratories LLC, and many other brand names of similar combinations are sold, including Vicodin and Lortab.

OxyContin (capitalized TWICE)

This is the trickiest one. OxyContin is a slow-release oxycodone preparation from Purdue Pharma LP. And, yes, the C is capitalized as well as the O. That's the way it's officially trademarked, so that's the way it should be written.

I have had officers practically plead to leave the C small, fearing it will be thought a typo by all who read their report. That may even be true, but without the additional, mid-word capitalization, the word is incorrect.

Any other examples of mid-word caps? While no longer in fashion, at one time many officers, including me, carried a BlackBerry!

hydrocodone (not capitalized)

A semi-synthetic opioid synthesized from codeine and an ingredient of several trademarked preparations, but not trademarked itself.

methadone (not capitalized)

Same as above. Often used to reduce withdrawal symptoms in heroin addicts.

Paxil (capitalized)

Paxil is a trademarked brand name for paroxetine, which, if prescribed in the generic form, is not capitalized. It is most often prescribed for depression and anxiety disorders.

Lipitor (capitalized)

Lipitor is prescribed for high cholesterol, similar to Zocor above.

metformin (not capitalized)

Perhaps the most common drug prescribed for Type II diabetes, not capitalized in this generic, chemical compound form.

Glucophage (capitalized)

Glucophage is a trademarked, brand name form of metformin.

marijuana (not capitalized)

As we hear so many times from defendants and supervisees with a positive drug test, "It's just a plant!" But the writing controversy for us is not so much in capitalization, but in spelling. In case you have not noticed, federal law often refers to the plant as "marihuana." How? Why?

Good question. According to John Hudak of the Brookings Institution, the plant was simply (and correctly) known as cannabis until unfortunate American resentment toward Mexicans and Mexican immigrants exploded after the Spanish-American War. Both spellings were common in Mexican Spanish at the time. By chance, it seems, the "h" version ended up being used in the Marihuana Tax Act of 1937.

Since the spelling is archaic and commonly used nowhere else, why is the marihuana spelling still there? Consider what it would take to change it: literally an Act of Congress. Unfortunately, there is no retired probation officer in the Capitol's basement with authority to scour the United States Code for archaic language and change it. In today's political atmosphere, can you imagine the public relations fallout for any elected official who introduced a bill to correct the spelling?

(Ominous voice) While Congresswoman Symington was wasting time debating how to spell marijuana, John Dudley was working hard in private industry bringing economic development home to . . ."

Don't look for it to change, in other words. When citing the actual code, quote it exactly as it is written. Everywhere else, spell marijuana correctly. That goes against the "stay consistent within a document" rule, but writing "Mr. Wheems has used marihuana since he was a teenager" isn't worth the consistency.

The best solution, of course, would be for us to adopt the actual name of the substance, like the rest of the world.

Cannabis.

antacid (not capitalized)

Antacid is the term for any substance that neutralizes acid in the stomach, usually a chemical base such as calcium.

codeine (not capitalized)

Common in prescription cough syrup, codeine is another opiate. It was first isolated in 1832 and is the most commonly taken opiate worldwide.

cocaine (not capitalized)

As opposed to the opiates, cocaine is a strong stimulant processed from the leaves of the coca plant. While the leaves have been chewed for centuries, the active compound was not isolated until 1855. Cocaine became very popular and was used both to treat heroin addiction and as an ingredient in a plethora of patent medicines. Pope Leo XIII was purportedly so fond of Mariani wine, a preparation laced liberally with cocaine, that he awarded its producer with a Vatican gold medal. And yes, cocaine really was an ingredient in the original Coca Cola. John Styth Pemberton's recipe included "a pinch of coca leaves" until 1906. Pemberton had suffered a saber wound in the Civil War and became addicted to opium. His "Pemberton's French Wine Coca" preparation resulted from his search for a cure.

Today we can't imagine a powerful stimulant being purposely added to a soft drink, can we?

By the way, a can of Diet Coke contains 42 milligrams of caffeine.

Asmacort inhaler (first word only capitalized)

Asmacort is a trademarked name for triamcinolone, used to treat asthma. An inhaler, though, is simply a delivery device, and is not capitalized. "Tylenol capsule" is a similar combination.

Theophylline (not capitalized)

Also an asthma drug, theophylline is produced under many trademarked brand names, but as a generic is not capitalized.

insulin (not capitalized)

Insulin is a natural substance produced by specialized cells found in the pancreas. It's interesting how insulin's connection to diabetes was discovered. In 1889, physician Oskar Minkowski removed a dog's pancreas to study the organ's role in digestion. He noticed flies were attracted to the dog's urine and discovered it to contain a high amount of sugar, suggesting something produced by the pancreas metabolized sugar. The world's first insulin injection was given to a 14-year-old boy in Toronto in 1922. The first American diabetic patient to receive insulin was a daughter of Charles Evan Hughes, former Governor of New York, secretary of state, and later chief justice of the United States Supreme Court.

That last bit of information is irrelevant to capitalization, but it indulges the former science teacher in me.

Narcan (naloxone hydrochloride) and Suboxone (a combination of naloxone and buprenorphine) are both trademarked drugs.

"Open up, Mrs. Shyster! It's the undersigned probation officer!"

4 LEGALESE IS A DISEASE

We see it all the time. In government and the legal community, inflated language is often the norm. Many of us learn to write legal documents by copying those written before, insuring that we continue the same tedious, overblown style. For example, a former-biology-teacher-turned-probation-officer once actually wrote the following sentence in an addendum to a presentence report:

Though the defendant's legal counsel examined the evidence in question and enumerated the individual marijuana plants he asserted met the standard of separate entities consisting of a root, stem, and leaf structure, the probation officer relies on the original count conducted by DEA investigators at the site of the crime while the plants were in their pristine state of plasmatic turgidity.

I am that probation officer.

Why does Mr. Jones reside at 200 Elm Street, instead of *live* there? Why does Ms. Smith increase her drug usage, instead of her drug use? Why does either of them purchase cocaine base, instead of buy it?

I think it's because we fear we will be seen as different, less sophisticated, and less competent if we write clearly and simply. That, friends, is a sad state of affairs.

Are we writing to impress the reader with our vocabulary? Or to convey meaning? Be brave! Be a trendsetter! Write clearly and concisely. Who knows? It may even catch on.

Let's begin with a simple exercise. Below are some of our favorite words. We use and read them every day. Let's see if there might be simpler, shorter, *clearer* ways to express their meanings. If so, write them to the right of each entry:

INSTEAD OF	*USE*
during the course of	
utilize	
analyzed	
reside	

INSTEAD OF	*USE*
marital union	
obtain	
purchases	
supplied	
prior to	
provided	
for the purpose of	
remained	
witnessed	
aforementioned	
procured	
ingested	
consumed	
forwarded	
usage	
adequate number of	

Was that easy? Probably. Then why do we use a longer, more complex, word when a shorter one can actually convey meaning more clearly?

While there are many possibilities, here are some options.

during the course of: during

utilize: use

analyzed: tested (if referring to a urine specimen, for example)

reside: live

marital union: marriage

obtain: get

purchased: bought

supplied: gave

prior to: before

provided: gave

for the purpose of: for *or* to

remained: stayed

witnessed: saw

aforementioned: *seldom necessary at all*

procured: got, bought

ingested: took, ate, drank, swallowed

consumed: took, ate, drank, swallowed

forwarded: sent

usage: use

adequate number of: enough

But I'm often told, "The words on the left just sound so much more *professional.*" I disagree.

The standard of our profession is to provide clear, concise, verified information in a form that can be used by all stakeholders. Everyone involved should be able to read your work quickly and easily. That mission does not mean leaving out pertinent information, but rather presenting it in the most easily used form.

Take *aforementioned*, for example. If a report refers to a particular car and then refers to the same car again later in the report, I assume "the car" is the same one without adding *aforementioned.* If it were a different car, and that were somehow important, you would tell me.

How is justice better served by saying a defendant *purchased* two OxyContin pills, instead of *bought* them? Will the judge be able to fashion a more just sentence? Will rehabilitation be more successful? Will the community safer because of it?

A marriage can be verified at the local courthouse. Do you really want to verify a *marital union*? Think about it. *Transported to police headquarters* conjures up the image of Scotty beaming a defendant straight into a holding cell. *Placed under arrest* instead of *arrested* serves what purpose? *The defendant was sweating and smelled of alcohol* gets the idea across quicker and just as clearly as *The defendant was perspiring profusely and emitted a strong odor of alcoholic beverages.*

Here are a few more overused words and phrases that sometimes make it into our writing and often into our speech, as well as a few that are just incorrect.

1. "In summary *or* summation" (If the reader can't tell that what he or she is reading is a summary, maybe the summary needs work.)

2. "Fairly unique" (Impossible – it's either unique or it's not.)

3. "I personally think" (You don't need "personally" because "I" already conveys who is doing the thinking.)

4. "At this moment in time" (Replace with "now" – using fewer words is usually better.)

5. "With all due respect" (Eliminate, since it's usually followed by a statement that is anything but respectful.)

6. "Absolutely" (I overuse this phrase and am working on reducing how many times I start my sentences with it, especially when responding to a question.)

7. "It's a nightmare" (Usually this phrase is an exaggeration – avoid it unless the seriousness of the situation truly warrants it.)

8. "Shouldn't of" (This is my personal pet peeve and I hear and see it everywhere - the correct phrase should be "shouldn't have.")

9. "24/7" (At one time, this may have been an interesting, unique phrase, but it has become so overused as to render it clichéd.)

10. "It's not rocket science" (Another popular variation is "it's not brain surgery" – reduce use of these phrases, because obviously, very little of our work is literally rocket science or brain surgery.)

The government website www.plainlanguage.gov has an excellent list of words and clearer, more concise possible substitutions, as well as many other great writing suggestions. Check it out.

FORMAL vs. INFORMAL WRITING

Another defense of our wordy, overblown legalese style I often encounter is as follows:

"But what we do is *formal* writing. We can't adopt an informal style for the court!"

I couldn't agree more. But before we assume we have conflict, let's look at the rules of formal writing style.

FORMAL WRITING CHARACTERISTICS

-Sentences are complex enough to add specific meaning to the writing.

-A sophisticated vocabulary, with terms that are accepted in the topic's field, is used.

-The tone is serious, and meanings are literal. There are no clichés or metaphors.

-The piece has a specifically stated purpose.

-Contractions are avoided.

-Punctuation, construction, and grammar follow standard rules.

-References are properly stated.

-Paragraphs are well organized.

-Slang and jargon are avoided. (Slang = a non-standard vocabulary composed typically of coinages, arbitrarily changed words, and extravagant, forced, or facetious figures of speech. Jargon = the technical terminology or characteristic idiom of a special activity or group.)

If you believe the first two items in the list mandate *resides* instead of lives, *placed under arrest* instead of arrested, *emitted a strong odor of alcoholic beverage* and *plasmatic turgidity*, well, bless your heart, as we say here in the South. Surprisingly, though, at the same time we battle hyper-formal legalese, writing that is too informal is also sometimes a problem.

EXERCISE: FORMAL vs. INFORMAL WRITING STYLE

Rewrite any of these sentences that contain informal writing style elements not acceptable for court reports (presentence, pretrial, supervision, memos, etc.).

1. The defendant would stay clean for a few months at a time and take her son back, then would go back into the drug scene.

2. After he found a job, he showed initiative from day one.

3. The defendant realizes that, at the end of the day, responsibility rests with himself.

4. His only job was at a Mickey D's in Dallas.

5. A K-9 unit was utilized and hit on a pair of sneakers in the defendant's closet.

6. He was revoked because of dirty urines.

7. A harsher sentence of incarceration is recommended because of the defendant's past failures while on paper.

8. The defendant has already washed out of two inpatient drug treatment programs.

9. While Mr. Jones is hooked on opiates, he will also smoke blunts whenever he can get them.

10. He started getting into trouble at age 13, at which time he started hanging around the pool hall his brother worked in.

Yes, all of these sentences came from actual reports that were either submitted to the court, or would have been submitted had they not been corrected. There are plenty of errors to choose from in these examples, but the use of slang and jargon is pretty plain. While the sentences can be rewritten any number of ways, we know *go back into the drug scene, from day one, at the end of the day, Mickey D's, hit on, dirty urines, while on paper, washed out, hooked on, blunts, and hanging around* are not acceptable in formal writing.

WHAT ABOUT *BUT, AND, I,* or *CONTRACTIONS?*

Some other elements of formal vs. informal writing many folks were taught in the past involved beginning sentences with *But, And, and I.*

Who would, in a court document, begin a sentence with *But* or *And*? No one, right? Take a look at this:

But the PROTECT Act was enacted without any consideration of the views of the Judiciary. It is, of course, the prerogative of Congress to determine what to consider in enacting a statute. But it surely improves the legislative process at least to ask the Judiciary its views on such a significant piece of legislation. And there can be no doubt that collecting information about how the Sentencing Guidelines, including downward departures, are applied in practice could aid Congress in making decisions about whether to legislate on those issues. And the Department can choose to appeal downward departures that it feels are unwarranted. But at least judges would have known that the process included a meaningful opportunity to have their views heard.

Heresy! Surely this couldn't be the writing of a learned, serious professional writing in an official capacity, right?

Admittedly, a few intervening sentences were removed from the passage to condense it, but the passage replicated above is from one page of late Chief Justice William Rehnquist's statutorily mandated *Annual Report on the Federal Judiciary* several years ago.

You can't get much more official than that. Pick up today's issue of the *Wall Street Journal.* Not exactly an edgy, libertine, throw-rules-to-the-wind publication, right? Look carefully, and chances are that you will find sentences beginning with *But* and *And.* I am not necessarily advocating the use of these words to begin sentences in reports or correspondence, but clearly those old rules regarding them are evolving.

Changes come to the judicial system very slowly. If you choose to use them and get questioned, refer to the venerable *Chicago Manual of Style*, not known as a leftist, bomb-throwing Bolshevik grammar scofflaw. It states, "There is a widespread belief—one with no historical or grammatical foundation—that it is an error to begin a sentence with a conjunction such as *and, but* or *so*. In fact, a substantial percentage (often as many as 10 percent) of the sentences in first-rate writing begin with conjunctions. It has been so for centuries, and even the most conservative grammarians have followed this practice."

One concession I do make to more formal writing (unlike this work) is avoiding contractions. They can still be acceptable depending on the overall tone of the document but are generally not used in our work.

The Gregg Reference Manual is against using contractions in formal writing, but *The Chicago Manual of Style* is less judgmental, stating they can sometimes help avoid really awkward sentences.

Of course, you do know that *o'clock* is a contraction, right? "The defendant returned to his residence at six of the clock." He was probably out checking his sibship.

Don't recognize *sibship?* You will soon.

IT'S TIME TO GET ACTIVE

Another archaic element of what was once considered formal writing is the use of *passive voice* instead of *active voice*. Here's the difference:

In most sentences with an action verb, the object of the sentence performs the action. In other words, the subject "acts upon" the verb. Examples:

The staff will attend writing training annually.

The public defender wrote lengthy objections.

Who is acting? The staff and the public defender. They are people or things *doing something.*

If, on the other hand, you said:

Writing training will be attended by the staff annually.

Lengthy objections were written by the public defender.

You would be using passive voice.

Unless there is some specific reason to do otherwise, you should write in active voice. *Someone is doing something.* Say it that way, instead of *something is being done to something by someone.* Let the actor and action be the focus, not what is being acted upon.

BOB, IS THAT YOU? OR THE UNDERSIGNED?

Another former rule of formal writing is to avoid using *I*, even when describing something the writer, clearly identified, did. Instead, we get sentences like this one, pulled from a memo:

On December 22, the Undersigned Probation Officer met with the defendant at his home, located at 428 Periwinkle Lane.

When I first became an officer and began reading and writing memos to the court, "the undersigned" struck me as strange, unnecessary, and awkward. It's not like the officer's name is a secret; it's right there on the page. I even saw it on memos with the officer's name in a block on the top and initialed, with no signature under the body of the letter at all, making it the Over-initialed Probation Officer, technically.

Not wanting to admit my lack of knowledge, I took a while to gather the courage to ask about it. The answer came without hesitation.

"Oh, there's a legal reason we have to do that."

"I see. What legal reason?"

-Pause-

"Yeah, legal. We have to write it that way because it's legal."

"But, what makes it not legal to say *I met with the defendant*, since I'm writing the letter, my name is on it, and I did it?"

-Pause-

"I think I left my gun locker key out in the car. I'll be right back."

I continued my quest and received similar results. Finally, I decide to write to the Assistant General Counsel of the Administrative Office of the United States Court. If there was, in fact, a legal reason to not use first person in correspondence, I wanted to know about it.

I framed the question with the example of a probation officer reporting a positive urine screen to the court and recommending no additional action because the offender had agreed to drug treatment. The correspondence included the sentence:

On July 14, the Undersigned Probation Officer collected a urine sample from Mr. Weeby at the offender's home, located at 229 Orion Lane.

I asked if a simple "I collected a urine sample" might not be acceptable, absent the illusive legal reason.

His verbatim response:

"You're correct – it's preferable for officers to write in plain English. Efforts to dress up the collection of urine with the gravitas of the third person are likely imitations of lawyers and other members of law enforcement who routinely dress up mundane matters with official-ese. No magic language is required or desired to get the idea across in a meaningful way. In addition, judges generally appreciate clearly written prose because they so rarely encounter it.

In sum, it's generally a bad idea to refer to oneself in the third person unless you are the Queen of England. Even then, the practice makes the writer or speaker sound silly and self-important, and that's never a good thing. Thanks."

So much for a legal reason.

(No offense to our lawyer friends, by the way, since the writer of that memo obviously is one himself.)

During the *Writing for Clarity* class, one Chief did say, somewhat resignedly, "But the Sisters told me it was impolite to use I. Not humble. Arrogant, even."

We are all results of our past, aren't we? But I really did collect that urine with great gravitas.

THE RUN-ON SENTENCE

Another problem sometimes found in our ponderous legal writing is the run-on sentence, which occurs when two or more sentences are punctuated and combined as if they were one.

There are two main types:

Fused sentences occur when two or more independent clauses "run together" with no punctuation. Commas and coordinating conjunctions are missing. Examples: *During my visit, the offender ate his dinner his son played quietly in the corner. He writes the reports she does the field work.*

Comma splices occur when two or more independent clauses follow one another and are incorrectly linked together only with a comma or commas. The coordinating conjunction is missing. Examples: *During my visit, the offender ate his dinner, his son played quietly in the corner. He writes the reports, she does the supervision.*

While comma splices may be somewhat less conspicuously incorrect than fused sentences, they are still to be avoided.

Strategies for Correcting Run-On Sentences

1. Insert a coordinating conjunction to create a compound sentence:

He writes the reports, and she does the supervision.

2. Insert a semi-colon:

He writes the reports; she does the supervision.

An even more common problem than run-on sentences:

While run-on sentences are fairly common, a bigger problem in court writing is known by the very technical term *Sentences That Are Just Too Dang Long.*

Another sentence taken straight from an actual court document:

As demonstrated through the interview with the defendant, in the presence of his attorney; collateral contact and verification attempts regarding the defendant's information/history; the independent gathering of offense reports, court documents, and other legal and/or relevant documents and the interview with family members, this officer attempted to relay all information provided by the defendant regarding his personal history, criminal history, and other relevant issues, in addition to the offense conduct and the advisory guidelines, to the Court.

That is one sentence of 77 words (unless I nodded off and miscounted). When I first read it, I wondered who was being punished: the defendant, or every single person tasked with reading the report. Does it have any elements that are technically incorrect? I'm afraid I can't answer that question. I have tried to do a word-for-word analysis, but before I finish, my mind drifts to life's brevity and the thought that I have not yet seen the Pyramids or the Aurora Borealis. Tempus fugit.

REDUNDANCY

I think we should eliminate, abolish, and wipe out redundancy.

Seriously, read a typical probation report of almost any kind, and you will find words that mean the same thing. All they do is clutter up meanings and add key strokes.

Some examples:

The defendant was represented by legal counsel.

This is from a criminal history section, describing a past conviction. What other sort of counsel are we likely to be talking about? Spiritual? Marital?

Bob Surly, age 42, lives with the defendant.

If a number is set off in commas after someone's name, it is going to be that person's age instead of his or her hat size or IQ. That's understood.

The defendant has a past history of heroin use.

So, I will describe that past history, and then I'll tell you about his present history and his future history? What other kind of history is there?

His drug use still continues. His drug use continues to this day.

If it continues, it continues. Period.

The case is still pending in state court.

Still pending, is it? If the Lincoln assassination case had not been settled, it would, even today, be just *pending.*

Pending is like flipping a switch, no matter how long a case lies without disposition. It either is, or it isn't.

REDUNDANCY EXERCISE

Revise these sentences, avoiding redundancy, wordiness, and passive voice.*

*This exercise was adapted from a similar one on Purdue University's Online Writing Lab (OWL) website, an excellent quick resource.

1. Some judges believe in capital punishment, while other judges are against it; there are many opinions on the subject.

2. In our district, there are wide-open opportunities for professional growth with an organization that enjoys an enviable record for stability in a dynamic atmosphere of community corrections.

3. In the not too distant future, probation officers must all become aware of the fact that there is a need for them to become acquainted with using GPS tracking technology.

4. The amendments that are considered most important by the Commission are those that have been shown to be needed by multiple instances of downward departure.

5. The community corrections conference was attended by more than a thousand probation officers and people in affiliated positions. After the subject of staff, salary, and benefit cutbacks came up, five participants were arrested for disorderly conduct by Metro Police, while several of the trainers and organizers were charged with organizing a public meeting without being issued a permit to do so. (Note: I'm glad I was not a facilitator at that gig!)

6. Trouble is caused when people disobey rules that have been established for the safety of all.

7. It is very unusual to find a defendant who has never told a deliberate lie on purpose.

8. There are many ways in which an assistant who is interested in meeting assistants from other districts may come to do so.

9. It is expected that the new urine collection schedule will be announced by the contractor within the next few days.

10. The defendant dropped out of school on account of the fact that it was necessary for him to help support his family.

11. Although the courthouse annex is populated by the probation office, close study of the building's safety has not been undertaken by the office's safety committee.

12. Many local law enforcement officers are planning to attend next Monday's meeting.

The deluge of overblown government writing is serious, so much so that it actually prompted legislation. The Plain Writing Act of 2010 was signed on October 13 of that year and reads, in part:

Beginning not later than 1 year after the date of enactment of this Act, each agency shall use plain writing in every covered document of the agency that the agency issues or substantially revises.

The Act only applies to the Executive Branch and, as I saw from all the correspondence I received from OPM and Social Security upon my retirement, it has been heartily adopted and is rigorously enforced.

Or perhaps not.

Still not convinced that simple, clear, writing is more professional?

While I was teaching this class in a big northern city some years ago, a magistrate judge came in to introduce himself, and, to my surprise, stayed for the class. During the first break, the room emptied of everyone but the two of us. He walked up, looked around, grabbed me by the arm and rather fiercely hissed, "Sibship!"

"Pardon me, Your Honor?"

"I said SIBSHIP."

"Judge, I'm sorry, but I don't understand."

"SIBSHIP! There's an officer in this class who uses that word in reports. MAKE HIM STOP!"

I had never heard it before that day, but sibship is indeed a word, defined as "a group of offspring having the same two parents; the state of belonging to a sib or having the same sib."

The defendant claims the following sibship: Leonard, a 46-year-old woodworker in Ann Arbor; Herschel, a 43-year-old florist in Holland…"

Don't use sibship.

Re-read this sentence from one of my early reports:

Though the defendant's legal counsel examined the evidence in question and enumerated the individual juvenile marijuana plants he asserted met the standard of separate entities consisting of a root, stem and leaf structure, the probation officer relies on the original count conducted by DEA investigators at the site of the crime while the plants were in their pristine state of plasmatic turgidity.

There is nothing glaringly incorrect in that sentence. The case involved marijuana plants that were discovered and plucked up while very young, and the defendant's lawyer disputed the number of plants. When I examined the evidence months later, it was hard for me to tell much from the brown, dried little mass of plants.

As a new officer, I felt this was an opportunity to impress with my plant expertise. I impressed, all right. The judge's law clerk called and said, "Danny, the judge would like to know what plasmatic turgidity *means*."

Impressive, right?

We are not meant to impress anyone with our writing. Our mission is to convey accurate information clearly and concisely. Our writing should go unnoticed, as the facts and analysis take center stage.

Face it. If anyone in the court notices your writing instead of the content, it's not likely to be in a positive way, now is it? Impress with credibility. Impress with knowledge. Impress with accuracy.

Impress with clarity.

EXERCISE

This passage is from an actual presentence report. Names and dates have been changed, but nothing else.

Rewrite the passage, and exchange your work with a coworker who has done the same. Proof each other's rewritten passage before returning them to discuss your changes and suggestions.

"According to the indictment on an unknown date in August 2025, in Burke County, East Augusta, the defendant did commit the offense of child abuse causing injuries by unlawfully and feloniously as the parent, guardian or custodian of a child, namely Darla Dalton, abusing said child and by such abuse did cause serious bodily injury to the child.

The defendant denied any suicidal ideation. He has a history of hospitalizations related to his mental health functioning and mental hygiene petitions. His most recent mental health evaluation was ordered by This Court. Based on a motion filed by the defendant's legal counsel, on October 15, 2024 the court-ordered the defendant be evaluated to make a determination concerning his mental health competency. He was sent to the Federal Medical Correctional Facility in New York, New York. On March 11, 2025, the Court did hold a competency hearing based on the results of the evaluation and adjudicated the defendant competent to assist in his own defense. However, the evaluation recommended a neurological assessment in order to rule out cognitive deterioration and evaluate the affects of the defendant's history of cranial trauma and stroke. On July 8, 2025, the United States Marshal's Service transported the defendant for said evaluation with Dr. Ahab Tincture a board certified Neurologist in Columbia, West Augusta. Dr. Tincture wrote to the Court stating that, after seeing the defendant, he would strongly discourage the use of the drug Dilantan and prescribe Topamaz and Lametal. The doctor further informed the Court that he could not make a determination concerning cognitive deterioration on the defendant because he was not a neuropsychologist, but that anyone with the defendant's past history of cranial trauma would expect their higher mental functioning to be effected. On July 18, 2025, a check with the Eastern Western Jail revealed that the defendant had not experienced any recent seizure activity and had adjusted well to the medication recommended by Dr. Tincture.

The defendant reported that he does not consume alcoholic beverages and has not drank said beverages in two years. He also indicated that he had not used marihuana in over one year. The defendant reported the only drug he was using was Xanax. He stated he illegally took this once per week for a two year period approximately two years ago. Previously prepared reports on the defendant indicated prior substance abuse history and problems. The defendant also denied ever receiving substance abuse treatment but records reflect that he did for a period of time in 2020, through Presidential Mental Health Center located in Washington, D.C."

Officer Kaine can split an infinitive at 25 yards.

5 ANTECENDENTS AND INFINITIVES

Antecedents

Antecedents and infinitives are probably terms you learned for a test in the seventh grade and promptly forgot. They really aren't complicated but are the source of many errors.

An antecedent is a word or phrase to which a pronoun refers. That definition might sound like double-talk, I know. It's best explained by example.

When you see the Chief, please tell her I'll be an hour late this morning.

Chief is the antecedent in this sentence. It is the word the pronoun *her* is referring to here.

But: When you see her, please tell the Chief I'll be an hour late this morning.

Here, the antecedent is still Chief, even though it comes after its pronoun *her.*

A problem often occurs in pronoun-antecedent agreement. The pronoun and antecedent must agree in number, gender, and person (first person, second person, third person). That requirement sometimes brings up something so difficult to correct that most of the time we don't even try.

Example: Anyone who uses illegal drugs is jeopardizing their future.

The word *anyone,* though it could randomly represent people among the 7.5 billion folks now inhabiting the planet, is grammatically singular. One.

The word *their* is plural, representing more than one. A sentence is like a mathematical equation in that both parts of it must be equal, at least in number. The example sentence just doesn't balance.

How to fix it? Unfortunately, English doesn't offer an easy, simple word substitution solution here. There is no one word that represents a singular version of *their* that is gender neutral. Commonly, we may hear *Anyone who uses illegal drugs is jeopardizing his future*, but we know that sentence leaves out half of the world's population!

How about *Anyone who uses illegal drugs is jeopardizing his or her future*? As clumsy as it may seem, that is correct. Singular pronouns come in two distinct gender varieties, and the language does not provide us with a unisex option. That's probably why the mistake is so often made.

Are there less awkward alternatives? How about *People who use illegal drugs are jeopardizing their future?*

People can be either singular or plural, so it works with the latter example. *Those* would work here as well.

Hm. Is that *their collective future*, or *their* i*ndividual futures* (plural)?

See why English is such a challenge?

ANTECEDENTS EXERCISE

Fill in the blank.

1. Each of the companies had ________________ books audited before the sentencing.

2. The supervision team was overworked, and ________________ fell behind.

3. The Safety Committee members put ________________ names on the policy.

4. If any one of the female officers needs a workout partner, ________________ can call me.

5. Neither the Chief nor the SUSPOs gave ________________ permission to provide refreshments.

Answers:

1. its (*each* is singular)

2. it (*team* is singular)

3. their

4. she

5. their*

* In sentences with both singular and plural compound subjects, such as example 5, use the pronoun consistent with the subject element closer to the verb.

Easy peasy, as our British friends would say, on the way to see the greengrocer.

A couple of basic rules:

1. Two or more subjects, whether singular or plural, joined by *and* act as a plural compound subject and take a plural verb. They write. The judge and the officer write.

2. Two or more singular subjects joined by *or* or *nor* act as a singular compound subject and take a singular verb to agree. The judge or the officer writes the order.

THAT DARNED THIS

I have heard some participants say that they were given the rule *Never begin a sentence with the word this.* That, like many rules, is much too broad, though I can see its intention. For example:

Mr. Smith has used cocaine for 20 years. This is why he cannot keep a job.

Why can't Smith keep a job? This. Not cocaine. *This.*

Here are some examples of how beginning sentences with *this* can be done, going from clear to shaky to murky.

1. To make the process quicker, we created a corporate presentence template. This template can be used to format new cases automatically. CLEAR - *This* refers back to a specific noun, *template.*

2. The Court orders supplies from a number of different vendors. This means that no one vendor has a monopoly over our purchasing options. SHAKY - *This* refers back to an entire sentence, not just one item.

3. We have ethics training quarterly, undergo background reinvestigations every five years, sign in and out of the office, have our inventory checked annually, and are evaluated twice a year. This keeps us honest. MURKY - *This* refers to a whole bunch of things, making it difficult for the sentence *This keeps us honest* to have specific meaning.

INFINITIVES

In most instances, an infinitive is a word pair beginning with *to* and ending with a verb. *To sleep, to eat, to write, to drive, to shoot* are all infinitives. They can be used as nouns, adjectives, or adverbs, but the issue that comes up most is the *split infinitive*, which occurs when you put an adverb between the word *to* and the verb in the pair. Using our examples above, *to deeply sleep, to greedily eat, to sloppily write, to drunkenly drive, and to accurately shoot* are all split infinitives.

He always tries to carefully check criminal records. Good for him! But now he should also try to avoid split infinitives. At first, that sentence probably sounds just fine to you. We use split infinitives in speaking so commonly that they sound perfectly natural.

Splitting infinitives sometimes does produce awkward sentences. The adverb often functions more effectively in another location.

When you are tempted to split an infinitive, instead try placing the adverb after the *object* of the infinitive (*presentence reports* in these examples):

The Judge asked you to thoroughly review these presentence reports. (Split infinitive)

The Judge asked you to review these presentence reports thoroughly. (Better)

If the first strategy doesn't work, try placing the adverb immediately before or immediately after the infinitive. But this approach may or may not produce a good sentence.

Examples:

I want you to personally supervise this defendant. (Split infinitive)

I want you personally to supervise this defendant. (Good)

I want you to supervise personally this defendant. (Not split infinitive, but an awkward sentence)

If steps one and two fail to produce an effective sentence, you may still have to split the infinitive. The Republic does not usually come to a screeching halt as a result, but it's still not good practice. It may be better to reword the sentence to avoid the infinitive altogether.

When an infinitive consists of *to be* and a past or present participle of another verb, inserting an adverb between *to be* and the participle is not considered splitting an infinitive; however, in many cases, you may be able to place the adverb more effectively elsewhere else in the sentence:

These records need to be thoroughly reviewed.

I will spare you any Shakespearian references concerning *to be* or not *to be.*

Split infinitives sometimes sound so natural that they are difficult to catch when reading. Maybe a little Baby Boomer trick will help:

PRACTICAL APPLICATION:

Here's a practical, easy way to check your work for split infinitives, and it involves *Star Trek*. Remember the introduction (I always considered it a soliloquy) from Captain Kirk at the beginning of the original series? Two things stand out in his last statement, the famous *To boldly go where no man has gone before.* "To boldly go" is a splint infinitive, Captain. So, when proofing a report, if you find a sentence that follows the *to boldly go* cadence, take a second look. A totally different issue is that the statement is sexist. There were women on the Enterprise. I know. Even though I was only six years old when it premiered, I noticed. And although the object of *before* is understood (Before us. Before now.), why was it omitted at the end of the sentence?

The *Star Trek* reference is often as good an indicator of the generational mix as the "Conjunction Junction" song. Gen Xers will note that Captain Picard did a bit better in *Star Trek: The Next Generation.* He removed the sexism (where no *one* has gone before), but sadly, held onto the split infinitive TO BOLDLY GO.

Transport me to the Courthouse, Scotty.

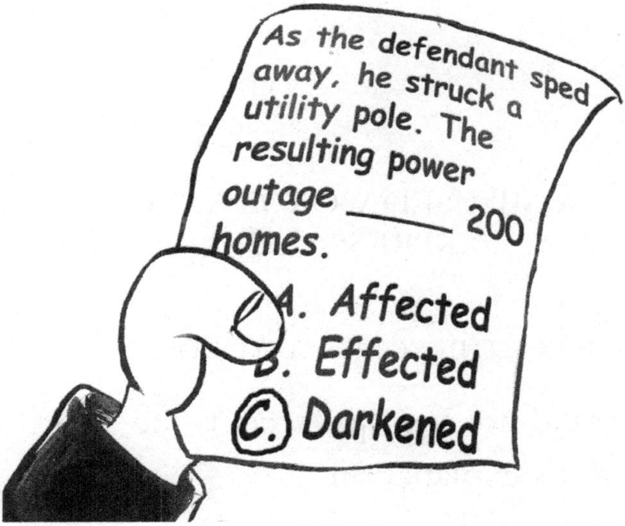
As the defendant sped away, he struck a utility pole. The resulting power outage ______ 200 homes.
A. Affected
B. Effected
C. Darkened

6 MISUSED WORDS AND EXPRESSIONS

UNDERLINE THE CORRECT WORD:

1. I could not (except/accept) the offender's explanation.

2. He was not (adverse/averse) to the idea of drug treatment.

3. We found everything (except/accept) the pepper spray.

4. The precursor chemical had (averse/adverse) (effects/affects) on the environment.

5. The cost will (effect/affect) the final urine screening contract.

6. We know that the (effect/affect) of the system breech will create problems.

7. The defendant found herself (between/among) several hostile detainees.

8. The agreement was made (between/among) two retained attorneys.

9. The corporation (apprised/appraised) the building in the fall.

10. John agreed to keep the Chief (apprised/appraised) of all changes in the case.

11. The defendant did his best to (assure/ensure) the officer that the test result was false.

12. The owners added a scaffold to (assure/ensure) that workers were safe.

13. The (bimonthly/semimonthly) supervision unit meeting occurs every other month.

14. A (biannual/semiannual) firearms inventory is produced twice a year.

15. The judge read the document and (censured/censored) objectionable parts.

16. The result of his misconduct was a vote to (censure/censor) the councilman.

17. We agreed that meeting deadlines was our (common/mutual) goal.

18. It was in the parties' (common/mutual) interest to reach an agreement quickly.

19. "This writing training wasn't as dull as I feared" is the highest (compliment/complement) I can receive.

20. The new subsidiary (complimented/complemented) the focus of the company.

21. The legal team is (comprised/composed) of staff members from three firms.

22. The legal team (comprises/composes) the top lawyers in the country.

23. The incidents occurred for three (consecutive/successive) months: June, July, and August.

24. The defendant's conduct continued over three (consecutive/successive) months: December, March, and July.

25. Mark's (continuous/continual) absence resulted in his termination.

26. Once started, the office coffeemaker will run (continuously/continually) until morning.

27. Both tried to be (discreet/discrete) about their romance.

28. The incidents occurred in three (discreet/discrete) periods.

29. The officers smelled marijuana on three (distinct/distinctive) occasions.

30. The defendant had a very (distinct/distinctive) voice.

31. Dr. Rogers was an (imminent/eminent) drug treatment specialist.

32. The crowd grew so unruly that violence was (imminent/eminent).

33. The two defendants were (exceedingly/excessively) happy with the verdict.

34. The two talked (exceedingly/ excessively) during the interview.

35. There were (less/fewer) field hours logged than the supervisor expected.

36. The amount of gasoline was (less/fewer) than we budgeted.

37. We decided to go (forward/foreword) with the project.

38. Most of the really valuable information is in the book's (forward/foreword).

39. The defendant set fires that were (obstacles/impediments) to the park's revenue.

40. The zoning law became an (obstacle/impediment) the builders could not overcome.

41. The minister's statement (inferred/implied) that he knew who had stolen the money.

42. We (inferred/implied) from Judge Keelor's statements that she was not happy with us.

43. We learned that, to find something quickly, we needed to look in the books' (indices/indexes).

44. The report listed the cost-of-living (indices/indexes) for 2020 and 2021.

45. I knew the holiday luncheon (preceded/proceeded) my teamwork presentation.

46. After the Judicial Conference approved the plan, we (preceded/proceeded) with the purchase.

47. The (principle/principal) reason we stopped using a contractor was the cost.

48. We did not want to pay, mainly because of (principle/principal) of the matter.

49. The courtroom was not easily (assessable/accessible) from the street.

50. The court budget will not be (assessable/accessible) for at least three months.

ANSWERS

1. accept
2. averse
3. except
4. adverse *and* effects
5. affect
6. effect
7. among
8. between
9. appraised
10. apprised
11. assure
12. ensure
13. bimonthly
14. semiannual

15. censored

16. censure

17. common

18. mutual

19. compliment

20. complemented

21. composed

22. comprises

23. consecutive

24. successive

25. continual

26. continuously

27. discreet

28. discrete

29. distinct

30. distinctive
31. eminent
32. imminent
33. exceedingly
34. excessively
35. fewer
36. less
37. forward
38. foreword
39. impediments
40. obstacle
41. implied
42. inferred
43. indexes
44. indices

45. preceded

46. proceeded

47. principal

48. principle

49. accessible

50. assessable

I'm sure you got all or almost all of these, because the reasons are often obvious when you take time to really consider them. One is *between* two others, while *among* many others. I'll keep you *apprised* as to when the house is *appraised.* *Consecutive* suggests uninterrupted succession, whereas *successive* means following in a regular sequence with one thing in relation to another. To *imply* is to hint as something, while to *infer* is to make an educated guess. The school *principal* is called that because she is the *principal* administrator in the school and follows the *principles* of fairness and compassion.

Some difficulty arises because, for most of us, the words are pronounced so similarly. Of course, pronunciation can vary, depending on from what part of the country you hail. For a Manhattan native, there are discernable differences in *Merry* and *Mary,* and between *pen* and *pin.* For me, a native of central

Appalachia, there are no differences. When we are rushed, we tend to write a word in the form we write it most often when translating it from our thoughts. Just recently, I looked back at something I had hurriedly scrawled and found "Your going to get a package from UPS later today." Big cringe!

Commonly misplaced by probation officers:

Keys Firearms Modifiers

7 AGREEMENTS AND MISPLACED MODIFIERS

Subject-verb number agreement may not be the greatest writing challenge we face, but sometimes plural words or singular words ending in *s* or intervening prepositional phrases can make us pause and think for a moment.

SUBJECT–VERB AGREEMENT EXERCISE

Circle the correct verb.

1. She and her fellow officers (is/are) taking defensive tactics class.

2. Either the pepper spray or the firearm (is/are) to be used in this scenario.

3. The defendant or his lawyers (run/runs) an illegal numbers scheme, while the lawyers or their client (run/runs) the rest of the office.

4. When it comes to investing in the C Fund, he (doesn't/don't), and they (doesn't/don't) either.

5. One of the UA boxes (is/are) leaking. The Chief, as well as her officers, (is/are) on the team.

6. Each one of those rounds (is/are) rusty.

7. The news from the Administrative Office (is/are) boring today. (Thank goodness!)

8. The shears (is/are) in the toolbox.

9. There (is/are) many questions still to be settled as a result of this decision.

10. The supervision team (run/runs) the

office. The family (has/have) four felons under one roof. My family (has/have) never been able to get past misdemeanors.

ANSWERS

1. *are* If the individual parts of a compound subject (consisting of separate elements *she* and *her fellow officers* in this example) are joined by *and*, use a plural verb.

2. *is* *Either* and *neither* are considered singular as subjects, but, if used as adjectives in either/or constructions, the number of the verb is determined by the number of the second noun, such as the singular *pepper spray* in this case.

3. *run* and *runs* Two or more plural subjects joined by any conjunction (*and, but, for, or, nor, so, yet*) take a plural verb. But if one or more singular subjects are joined to one or more plural subjects by *or* or *nor*, the verb agrees with the subject closest to the verb.

4. *doesn't* and *don't*

5. *is* and *is*

6. *is* One is singular, and *each one* refers to all the rounds in the group, *individually*.

7. *is*

8. *are* American English almost always treats collective nouns (such as *mob, gang, group, herd,* and *pack* for example) as singular, so a singular verb is used with them. On the other hand, nouns representing objects with two parts, such as *shears* and *scissors*, require plural verbs. But when referring to a *pair* of something, use a singular verb. The *shears* are in the toolbox. The *pair of shears* is in the toolbox.

9. *are* In sentences beginning with *There*, the verb, whether singular or plural, is determined by whether the noun *after* the verb is singular of plural.

10. *runs, has*, and *has* *Team* and *family* are considered collective nouns and are treated as singular.

THE DANGLERS AND THE MISPLACED

Dangling Participles is another term you may remember hearing, but seldom apply to your own writing. I am a big fan of dangling participles mainly because they offer a great opportunity for humor.

Every verb has forms called participles. For many regular verbs, adding *–ed* gives you the past participle, and adding *-ing* gives you the present participle. *Yesterday I laughed. Today I am laughing. Yesterday I helped. Today I am helping.* Of course, there are many verbs with past participles that do not follow the *–ed* extension, such as *shot, brought,* and *sung.*

A participle is said to be dangling when it is intended to modify a noun that is not actually present in the text.

Dangling participles and other misplaced modifiers (phrases or clauses placed awkwardly in a sentence so that they appear to modify or refer to an unintended word) can conjure up some incredible images.

Driving down Forrester Street, the offender's house came into view.

I spotted the firearm walking into the courtroom.

The office refrigerator held urine samples from 12 offenders frozen in the top compartment.

The defendant was walking a dog with an electronic monitoring unit on his ankle.

We saw several lawyers looking out our office window.

While trying to get ready for court, the telephone rang continually.

We could see marijuana growing from our car window.

I found a summons in the mailbox that doesn't belong to me.

The suspect was about 20 years old, Caucasian, 6", with wavy hair weighing about 180 pounds.

You get the idea. Houses shouldn't be driving anywhere, even down Forrester Street. Firearms do not walk. We do not freeze offenders. Dogs don't wear our EM units. Lawyers have their own windows to peer through. Telephones don't get ready for court. Marijuana doesn't grow on car windows. We don't look into anyone's mailbox but our own. Suspects lugging around 180 pounds of hair can't get very far.

The defendant was found guilty and sentenced to life in federal court.

Admittedly, I have had a few days in court that felt like they lasted a lifetime. Perhaps you have, too.

My favorite example sets up a scenario that could be a bit unsettling for people in our profession:

While getting my newspaper early Sunday morning, I saw the fugitive standing on the porch in my pajamas.

What he was doing in my pajamas, I'll never know.

Officer Jenkins verifying a marital union.

8 MISCELLANY

So many little things come up in our work. That's what makes it a *unique profession*, as the Charter says. Consider this chapter that "catch-all" drawer in your desk that you go to when you can't find something you seldom use.

WHO/WHOM

See if you can replace the word *who* with *he* or *she.* If not, see if you can replace it with *him* or *her.* If you can use *he* or *she*, that's the time for *who.* If it needs to be *him* or *her*, use *whom.* If one of the words is a sentence's subject (instead of an object), it will be *who.*

Who would like to earn comp time this evening?

That's correct. He would. She would. (*Him would* and *Her would* will not work, so *whom* is eliminated.)

You spoke to the lawyer and then the defendant. Whom do you believe?

That is also correct. I believe him. I believe her. (*I believe he* or *I believe she* will not work, so *who* is eliminated.)

THAT PERSON ENGAGED TO BE MARRIED

A man who is engaged to be married and a woman who is engaged to be married are, believe it or not, two different things.

He and his (fiancée/fiancé´) have cohabited for 12 years and have 8 children.

A *fiancée* is a woman. A *fiancé* is a dude.

YOU AND I AND ME MAKE THREE

Please notify Carol or myself when asking for a continuance. The Judge told Megan and I to leave.

Both sentences are incorrect. If you and another person are in a sentence, use the same pronoun for yourself that you would use if the other person were not there. You would not say, "Please notify *myself* when asking for a continuance. The Judge told *I* to leave the courtroom." It's *me*.

THE GREAT HOWEVER

Is it correct to begin a sentence with *However*?

Boy, is this one of our favorite things! There is good news and bad news.

First, the good news: Yes, under certain circumstances, it is correct form to begin a sentence with *However.*

The bad news: the correct usage is illustrated in this sentence:

CORRECT: However you divide the budget, there will not be enough money for new vests.

When *However* begins a sentence, it means "in whatever way" or "to whatever extent."

INCORRECT: The defendant has been married three times. *However,* all his marriages were in different states, and he has never been widowed or divorced.

Strunk and White's *The Elements of Style* gives definitive guidance in the *however* matter.

WELL, THERE IS THAT

Just because something is not technically incorrect does not mean it's good writing. I think we have all determined *that.*

In some documents, the word *that* could be used half as much, and the overall effect would be an improvement. Sometimes the word *that* is necessary, but just as often it is not.

When to use *that*:

That is frequently used to attach a dependent clause to an independent clause.

That is necessary if a clause begins with certain subordinating conjunctions, such as *before, while,* and *in addition to.*

That should be used before clauses that clarify a noun.

That is clarifying after certain verbs and verb phrases, such as *contend, estimate,* and *point out.*

And, sometimes, a sentence just sounds awkward without *that*, so put it in when your ear dictates.

Use *that* in sentences like these:

He said *that*, although a new G-car sounded like a good idea, continuing the drug treatment contract with the year-end money sounded even better.

The notion *that* the recidivism rate will further decrease under these circumstances is laughable.

When to leave *that* out:

You can usually drop *that* if it follows a verb when it essentially means "to say." Doing so usually sounds natural when read aloud.

The officers claimed fit time would raise their productivity. (No need for "claimed *that* fit time.")

She insisted she wasn't responsible for the trash left in the G-car. (No need for "insisted *that* she wasn't.")

But if other words come between the verb and the dependent clause (a clause that cannot stand as a sentence on its own), it's often better to keep *that*. Again, reciting the sentence aloud can be helpful.

The officers also said *that* a compressed work schedule would reduce absenteeism.

She admitted reluctantly *that* she had gone through the McDonald's drive-through on the way back to the courthouse.

You can also usually omit *that* if it would precede a simple relative clause.

Neither of them was particularly pleased with the compromise they had reached. (No need for *the compromise that they had reached.)*

What about twice in a row? Even spell check chokes on repeated words, but it's sometimes technically correct to use *that* twice, though should be creatively avoided if possible.

He confessed *that that* robbery had been planned over the past three months.

Better: He confessed that, over the past three months, that robbery had been planned.

This example assumes the conversation may involve more than one robbery, and the confession in question pertained only to a particular felonious incident. Otherwise, *He confessed that the robbery had been planned over the past three months* would be better still.

THAT vs. WHICH

Sometimes reducing *that* means just replacing it with *which.* Be careful, because the meaning can change.

The first defensive tactics class that all the officers attended was free of injuries.

The first defensive tactics class, which all the officers attended, was free of injuries.

The two sentences do not mean exactly the same thing. In the first sentence, a specific group of officers attended the class for the first time. In the second sentence, the fact that all the officers attended is a less significant detail.

The difference may seem inconsequential, but it determines the correct word choice. It has to do with what are known as *restrictive* and *nonrestrictive* relative clauses. We made reference to clauses in our comma exercise, because they can also affect comma placement.

A *restrictive relative clause* contains essential information about the noun that comes before it. If you leave the clause out, the meaning of the sentence is affected. The sentence might be easily misunderstood or make no sense at all.

Example:

He held out the finger that was hurt.

In this sentence, *that* is introducing (comes before) a restrictive relative clause (was hurt).

A *nonrestrictive clause*, on the other hand, contains extra information that could be left out of the sentence without affecting the meaning. Nonrestrictive relative clauses can be introduced by such words as *which, whose, who*, or *whom,* but not by *that.*

He held out his finger, which the doctor examined.

He held out his finger is a perfectly fine sentence. *Which the doctor examined,* of course, is not, but it does offer quite a bit of additional information.

He held out his finger, **that** *the doctor examined* does not work.

The very best explanation comes from the *Chicago Manual of Style*, because it involves something so appropriately associated with Chicago itself. Pizza!

"Pizza that's less than an inch deep just isn't Chicago-style."

In this example, removing *that's less than an inch deep* leaves you with an inaccurate sentence. What do you mean, *Pizza just isn't Chicago style?* The phrase is restrictive, so *that* is used.

Pizza, which is a favorite among Chicagoans, can be either bad for you or good, depending on how much of it you eat.

In this sentence, taking out *which is a favorite among Chicagoans* still leaves you with a sentence that makes sense. *Pizza can be either bad for you or good, depending on how much of it you eat.* I can't argue with that premise. The phrase is nonrestrictive, so *which* is used.

HYPHENS

Like many things in our profession, hyphen use can be grey instead of black-and-white. There are many, many rules, but just a few cover most situations.

A compound adjective is a combination of words acting as a single idea that modifies a noun. If it comes before the noun, it is often hyphenated.

The new firearms simulator used state-of-the-art technology. (Here, four words are acting as an adjective modifying *technology* and are hyphenated.)

But if the compound adjective comes after the noun it modifies, the adjective is usually not hyphenated.

The new firearms simulator's technology is state of the art.

Hyphenated ages

Hyphens are often used in ages unless the period of time is written in plural form.

The defendant has a five-year-old daughter.

But no hyphens in *The defendant's daughter is five years old* because *years* is plural.

Sometimes, as with many other writing elements, hyphens may be used when omitting them can be confusing. *The defendant has a concealed-weapons permit* is clear. While *The defendant has a concealed weapons permit* is not likely to be taken as "She has a permit, and keeps that permit hidden," it could technically be interpreted that way.

Hyphenate prefixes when they come before proper nouns or proper adjectives. A *proper noun* is used for an individual person, place, or organization spelled with initial capital letters. *Bob, Great Britain, Chicago Cubs.* A *proper adjective* is an adjective that is a name derived from a proper noun, and is usually capitalized. *American cheese, Canadian bacon, Shakespearian play.*

Example: We usually schedule our district retreats for mid-September.

Hyphenate compound numbers, twenty-one through ninety-nine.

The package contained *fifty-seven* pills.

SPEAKING OF NUMBERS

There are differences among style guides on how to write numbers, so make a point to refer to the one you have chosen for your office.

One simplified rule is to spell out numbers expressed in one or two words, and use figures for other numbers.

Examples:

more than ten pounds of marijuana

less than thirty thousand pills

twenty-three other racketeering defendants

after 120 days

more than 350 doses

It is not good practice to use numeric expressions to begin as sentence.

Avoid: 100% of his post-conviction urine screens tested positive for cocaine.

Avoid: All of his post-conviction urine screens tested positive for cocaine. *or* The percentage of his urine screens that tested positive for cocaine was 100%.

Generally, do not mix written numbers and numeric expressions in the same sentence.

Incorrect: The defendant had taken two OxyContin, 12 Vicodin, and an aspirin.

But sometimes it may be necessary to mix numerical forms in order to avoid confusion:

The geriatric incarceration section housed 110 90-year-old prisoners. (Definitely write one of these out. *The geriatric incarceration section housed 110 ninety-year-old prisoners* is much less likely to be misunderstood.)

TIME AFTER TIME

If a crime occurred at exactly 12:00, and it's dark outside, how would you report the time? That question gets quite a bit of discussion, and I'm not surprised, because this time is recorded incorrectly almost everywhere. A quick look at your local TV listings will provide examples.

There is no such thing as 12:00 AM or 12:00 PM. They do not exist. Sure, there is a 12:01 AM and a 12:01 PM, but not 12:00 on the button. So, if that 911 call came in at precisely 12:00, and it was dark, it was *midnight.* If the sun was shining, it was *noon.*

Then why not refer to 12:00 midnight, or 12:00 noon? The numbers in these cases are redundant. I mean, what other midnight is there, but the one at 12:00?

Is 12:01 when it's dark outside PM or p.m.? The latter has been the standard for decades because it is an abbreviation, but PM and AM are becoming acceptable. Just make sure you are consistent throughout your document. The same, by the way, pertains to state abbreviations. My home state is still sometimes written *W.Va.,* but *WV* is becoming more common, and *DC* is seen just as frequently as *D. C.*

"No, I'm not the investigating officer. I'm the grammar police. May I see your report, please?"

9 EVEN MORE COMMA SENSE

Commas are so important and the source of so much controversy that we will give them a second look, this time using a different set of comma rules and examples in order to both give you a refresher and cater to different learning styles. For some of you, it may seem disconcerting to see the rules stated so differently, but the exercise is designed that way to help you focus on organic application rather than rule interpretation, because those rules vary from manual to manual.

1. Use a comma when two sentences are joined with *and, but, or, nor, yet, so,* or *nor.*

2. Use commas to separate three or more elements in a series.

3. Place a comma between two consecutive adjectives that describe the same noun.

4. Separate unrelated numbers with a comma if it clarifies the numbers. Put commas in numbers with four or more digits.

5. Use commas to separate parts of dates and addresses.

6. Place commas after most introductory words or phrases.

7. Use commas to set off elements providing additional information that could be omitted without changing the meaning of the sentence.

8. Use commas to separate transitional expressions when the flow of the sentence is interrupted.

9. Use commas to set off a word or phrase that renames a noun or pronoun that comes before it.

10. Use a comma to set off contrasting elements that are not essential to the meaning of a sentence.

11. Insert commas to help avoid confusion.

12. Use commas to enclose nouns or pronouns used as direct address.

EXERCISE

Punctuate these sentences. Some sentences may not need additional punctuation.*

*Adapted from www.businesswriting.com, © The Business Writing Center

1. It is within performance goals that teams become a primary form of organization but questions of alignment coordination and control arise.

2. Six areas of weaknesses experienced by organizations are dependence on quality of leadership fragile motivation loss of some managerial control volatile earnings loss of specialization and a shift in loyalty.

3. We pride ourselves on giving generous fringe benefits.

4. We try to promote young talented people.

5. Results indicated invoices from $10000 to $70000 were listed.

6. The invoice numbers included 1938734 to 1938798.

7. The training began in September 2021 and did not meet the desired goal.

8. Even after all they accomplished it still didn't seem fair for everyone.

9. A manager who puts off a decision that will affect the work of other people is waffling.

10. In practice however if all goes well routine meetings will take care of themselves.

11. When the entire class formed study groups known as "sections" Charles finally felt a sense of belonging.

12. The group consisted of achievers not performers and their work was well written.

13. By noon interest in the project was gone.

14. To do this of course it is essential to understand the professional long-range requirements.

I hope those sentences were difficult to read, because many of them are examples of horrible writing. By now, you know they are rife with problems, including poor structure, improper antecedents, passive voice, and a host of other issues in addition to the comma mistakes. But for now we will only concentrate on commas.

Let's see how close your revisions are to mine.

1. It is within performance goals that teams become a primary form of organization, and questions of alignment, coordination, and control arise.

2. Six areas of weaknesses experienced by organizations are dependence on quality of leadership, fragile motivation, loss of some managerial control, volatile earnings, loss of specialization, and a shift in loyalty.

3. We pride ourselves on giving generous fringe benefits.

4. We try to promote young, talented people.

5. Results indicated invoices from $10,000 to $70,000 were listed.

6. The invoice numbers included 1,938,734 to 1,938,798.

7. The training began in September 2021 and did not meet the desired goal.

8. Even after all they accomplished, it still didn't seem fair for everyone.

9. A manager who puts off a decision that will affect the work of other people is waffling.

10. In practice, however, if all goes well, routine meetings will take care of themselves.

11. When the entire class formed study groups known as "sections," Charles finally felt a sense of belonging.

12. The group consisted of achievers, not performers, and their work was well written.

13. By noon, interest in the project was gone.

14. To do this, of course, it is essential to understand the professional, long-range requirements.

Are our answers 100% the same? Not likely, but don't worry. Compare the two sets of sentences to see if you agree with the answers. Most likely any discrepancy was an oversight, but if not and you can justify your comma decision using one of the rules, you have done well. Practicing the process and being able to justify answers are our goals. Remember, grammar is like the law, and at least in this respect, we are judges, or at least lawyers who can reasonably argue interpretation.

Why did we just use such perfectly wretched pieces of writing? Each of these sentences appeared in actual business correspondence or reports compiled by the The Business Writing Center, a company that does a brisk international business teaching on-line writing classes. It should give us a little comfort to know we are not so bad off after all, and that everything we have discussed applies to the private sector as well as to us. We are not alone.

"Sorry Watkins, but a class B felony report has to weigh 14 ounces, minimum."

10 PUTTING IT ALL TOGETHER

So much stuff! But most of what we have discussed is intuitive, and you get almost everything right in your writing most of the time. You are a great writer in a very important field, and now, I believe, you will be even a little better.

The potential for improvement in clarity is great. I hope you will begin looking at the work of others a bit more critically as well, not to be smug or condescending, but to compare and find ways to continue to improve your own writing.

For example, as I was writing the original course, I decided to critically review the very next memo that came to my desk. It just so happened the memo was a one-pager from Washington, on the topic of remote access devices. I no longer even remember who authored it, and no disrespect is intended, because the memo is no better or worse than any other I received over the years.

Here it is:

The ability to remotely access our electronic records has become an expectation rather than the exception over the past several years. Approximately 10,000 of us carry Blackberry's or other handheld devices, not to mention all of the laptops that are used on travel and from home. These devices provide employees with the capability to do everything from accessing their e-mail and desktop applications to surfing the Internet. However, with all this productivity enhancing functionality comes attendant risks and responsibilities, and the risk goes far beyond any individual user's device or data. The potential to adversely impact the entire organization is all too real. Additionally, these devices are Judiciary resources and each of us is responsible for their appropriate use.

Judiciary staff now routinely use remote access devices to access and transmit sensitive information both over the Internet and the Judiciary's private network. As a result, it has become critically important that we employ appropriate security techniques such as adequate strength passwords and encryption capabilities. Every user of a Judiciary supplied remote access

device (Blackberry, smart phone, iPhone, PDA, laptop, etc.) needs to regularly review their remote access practices to ensure they are safe, secure and responsible.

This is just another memo from back when the BlackBerry was more popular, right? It gets its meaning across.

But it could easily be used as an exercise illustrating so many of the rules we have discussed. The BlackBerry smartphone, like OxyContin, is a trademarked word with two capital letters. *However* begins a sentence. Every user (singular) needs to regularly review their (plural) practices. And *to regularly review*? Remember to boldly go? Split infinitive. Ensure your practices are safe, secure and responsible. So, secure and responsible are a single term, unequal to safe? Where is the Oxford comma?

With all this productivity enhancing functionality comes attendant risks…

It would take more than just the missing hyphen to improve this pristine state of plasmatic turgidity, I'm afraid. And, there are many more such issues just in this one memo alone.

Be brave. Be professional. Be a trendsetter. Write clearly. When you read something, think *How could this be better?* And then apply your answers to your own work. Have a conversation about writing quality with your supervisors, with your support staff, with the people you supervise, and yourself.

Our work is too important to do otherwise. While we fumble for meaning in layers of mediocre writing, more important things await.

THE FINAL EXERCISE

I promise!

On your own paper, correct the following sentences, and if necessary, revise them to convey as clearly as possible all the information they contain. Use all resources available, including other references, etc.

1. The program gives preference to individuals that have GED's.

2. According to the indictment on an unknown date in August 2021, in Burkes County, West Augusta, the defendant did commit the offense of child abuse causing injuries by unlawfully and feloniously as the parent, guardian or custodian of a child, Jude Smith, abusing said child and by such abuse did cause

serious bodily injury to the aforementioned child.

3. The defendant has previously maintained residences in Columbus, Ohio, Portsmouth, Ohio and Huntington, West Virginia.

4. Ms. Smith was married in 2021 to Bob Jones, who is currently 47 years of age and resides in Reno, Nevada.

5. Mr. Jones stated he has no past history of mental health treatment. There is no documented evidence to suggest other wise.

6. The evaluation took place at the office of Dr. Bob Smith located in Mobile, Alabama.

7. Upon the trooper's arrival at the residence, Mr. Blevins rendered a statement to the trooper claiming ownership of the reported stolen

firearms and he surrendered the remaining firearm he had in his possession, a .22 caliber bolt action rifle, bearing serial number 53965, to the trooper.

8. Subsequent to his divorce, the defendant's drug usage increased.

9. The officers utilized a drug dog in the execution of the search.

10. His mother is sixty one and is employed by the Oneida County Board of Education as a School Cook.

11. He retrieved a large plastic baggie of alleged marihuana from a hidden compartment located in close proximity to the kitchen stove. The defendant then sold the CI an amount of alleged marihuana in exchange for $25.00 in prerecorded United States Currency.

12. The U. S. Marshal's Service transported the defendant to the Summit County jail.

13. The defendant appears to be at low risk of non appearance.

14. At present, the main tie the defendant has to the community are her family members including her parents and sisters.

15. Ms. Fife attends classes Monday thru Thursday from 7:30 am to 12:00 pm.

16. Her current residence is owned by her parents. Prior to this, the defendant resided at Post Office Box 734 in Lake Huron, Michigan, for one year. Prior to this, she resided on Water Street in Bennington, Vermont for one year. Prior to this, she resided at Route 2 Box 23a there for twenty years. Prior to this, she resided with her parents in Dover, NH.

17. Ms. Hummel takes a variety of prescriptions, including Wellbutrin, Klonopin, Oxycodone, Ambien, Diuretic, and an Epinephrine pin.

18. The defendant's personal information is based on information provided by the defendant. Computer inquires with criminal and driver's history databases confirmed his numeric identifiers and residential address.

19. Mr. Jones has two children, Albert Jones, age 4, and Nevaeh Jones, age 3, whom reside with their mother, Kelly Smith, in Evergreen, Washington.

20. Mr. Treasly is currently unemployed.

21. Mr. Rice is a male Caucasian who stands 5'11" tall, weighs 155 lbs. has brown hair hazel eyes and a tattoo of a shamrock on his left arm.

22. Mr. Flam has no other tattoos or scars to report.

23. Waived to Circuit Court, charges still pending.

24. Mr. Phibes is a life long resident of Lee County.

25. The recommended conditions should insure the defendant's appearance for court hearings.

26. The defendant went to school through the 8th grade but did not finish due to non-attendance and dropping out.

27. Found in the closet was a 20 gage shotgun.

28. Ms. Wannamaker described other times where Ms. Buckland had seen her on the street and told her she was going to get her.

29. One of the officer's dressed himself up as a delivery man from Airborne and along with a surveillance team, they went to the address at 397 Oiler Avenue.

30. The defendant reports he worked for Show-me Carnival Company, based out of Atlanta, Georgia.

31. His siblings include Bert, who lives in Florida and works at McDonalds, and Carl, who lives in Memphis, Tennessee, where he owns his own business.

32. The defendant is a lifelong resident. He has apparent familial and property employment ties to the local community. There are no apparent indicators to suggest the defendant poses a risk of non-appearance.

33. The defendant has one historical DUI offense.

34. Stolen property recovered by the investigators included forty two collectors coins, nine whisky decanter's and a hopper video recorder.

35. The defendant was sentenced to 12 months imprisonment and 36 months supervised release.

36. During the chase, the car crashed into a utility pole, effecting electrical service to over two hundred customers.

37. Mr. Starks' mother, Elizabeth Starks, died in 1913, following the loss of a battle with cancer.

38. Mr. McNeer also reported for the past year, he stays approximately five nights per week with Shelby Kitchen, a friend, in Butte, Montana, and occasionally with his maternal half sister, Tiera White, in Helena.

39. Ms. Pike suffers from having Multiple Sclerosis, Musculoskeletal Pain, and a low pulse rate. She is prescribed numerous medications, including Nitroglycerin.

40. She is a long term resident of this district, and has apparent familial and emotional ties to the local community.

41. Even though for his age, the defendant has an extensive history of criminal arrests, of which he is being cut a huge break for the state dismissing all of his pending charges, a sentence of fifteen years seems long enough for the instant offense.

42. The defendant was interviewed in the U. S. Marshalls Service lockup.

43. The defendant was represented by legal council, Bob Oldham.

44. Prior to the search, the defendant had told officers of the white bag with a shoe box inside, but he said he never knew what was inside the shoe bag.

45. Mr. Smith reported that prior to his arrest, he used alcohol socially, but never had felt like it caused him any problems.

46. Mr. Overine cohabitates with his fiancé, Lucy Luster.

47. Mr. Forrest Gimp uses crutches to assist him in his mobility.

48. His offspring include Bob, a carpenter in Pachuta, Mississippi and Clarence, who is a soldier enlisted in the United States Army and currently serving in the middle east.

49. His monthly income consists of $1300, received for his performing odd jobs. Assets include a boat valued at $3500, that the defendant purchased in approximately 2024.

50. The marital union produced the following issue: Ham, currently age 4, Sham, currently age 6, Japhat, currently age 8, and Larry, currently age 10.

Now, exchange your revisions with another person completing the exercise and compare them. Set aside some time for later discussion. For many sentences, there are several avenues for improvement and is no single right answer.

Yes, all those sentences, too, came directly from actual probation/pretrial documents, with identity/location protection changes. Did any of them make you smile and think, "I have seen those very words. Have I even written some of them myself?" I suspect so, and there is no shame in it. None of us are satisfied with our skill levels the first day we enter our profession. Daily improvement is important to justice, rehabilitation, and safety, including our own.

Will improving your writing take more time in your already busy day? Yes, I am afraid it will, *at first.* But since the days of handing a dictated tape to a typist are long over, improving your writing will, eventually, save you time. Think of the number of keystrokes saved in a tight, concise report. Think of the time saved going right to the heart of a thought, without all the *pristine states of plasmatic turgidity* and the *productivity enhancing functionality* getting in the way of the necessary information.

A NOTE ON EMAIL

Just before retiring, I received an email from an officer in another state doing courtesy supervision on one of our cases.

Drug test conducted this date and sent off for confermation, test results looked like it was positive for marijuana but it was vaque so I sent if off.

For some people, email often assumes more relaxed communication rules than hard copy correspondence. Should those relaxed rules be acceptable in our work communication? The email above was still official government correspondence about an important subject that could affect someone's freedom and the community's safety. Would it be possible that some turn of events could have me distributing copies of that email to lawyers and testifying to the message's content? That scenario is unlikely, but not impossible. If you are writing as part of your official duties, please remember how important your words *and your readers* are to the judicial system.

Where to go from here? I am glad you asked.

PLANNING YOUR OWN WRITING IMPROVEMENT PROJECT

Take an objective look at the writing in your organization. The writing may already be great. Could it be better? The answer is always yes, so you may wish to consider your own writing improvement project.

STEP 1: COMMIT

There is no use beginning if you do not have the commitment to follow through. Let everyone, including the judges, know you are looking at writing across the district and are hoping to make improvements. Ask the judges if there are particular problem areas they have noticed. Create a writing improvement committee and ask for volunteers. Make sure all the areas are represented, from receptionists to IT specialists to managers.

STEP 2: GATHER EXAMPLES

One of the biggest problems in an organization's written communication is a lack of consistency. No, that doesn't mean you should develop boilerplate language for every contingency and be intolerant of style differences. But gathering a few representative samples from each division and office in your district will likely impress you with the *diversity* and *creativity* in the way grammar rules are followed. (How's that for positive spin?)

STEP 3: DECIDE ON A REFERENCE

No one wins in a battle of dueling writing manuals. Decide on one definitive reference and get a copy for each committee member (or at least one per divisional office). Make sure everyone has access to official report writing monographs and uses those as example as well, even though you will find inconsistencies in them once you look closely.

STEP 4: RECRUIT PROOFERS

Have committee members proof the assembled reports and correspondence, using official report monographs and your chosen style manual as references. Ask each member to keep running lists of the most common errors. The lists they develop should come with examples lifted from the documents, but assure them they only need to list recurring errors, not every single thing they correct. In six months' time, a typical supervisor may correct a hundred comma errors, but just a few examples showing the most common varieties will suffice. Give reminders and encouragement (I find donuts work especially well with probation and pretrial services staff) along the way.

STEP 5: Collect the error lists from all your committee members, and have the committee meet to discuss them together. Using the chosen reference, the committee should agree on corrections and preferred practices.

STEP 6: Who drew the short straw to develop and conduct the training? Your training coordinator most likely, but the program could be a great opportunity bring another person into the staff development fold as well. The training does not have to be elaborate or replete with bells, whistles, and fireworks. *Writing for Clarity* certainly isn't flashy, but the applicability should be obvious, because the program sprang from actual examples gathered from the participants themselves. How much more relevant can a training program be than one based your own words?

STEP 7: Assemble the committee and present the new training program to its members first. The program will give you the opportunity to work out any problem areas. Encourage members to ask any questions they anticipate may come from their staff.

STEP 8: Conduct the training, and ask for feedback from the participants. Ask proofreaders to assess whether or not they see improvement over the next few weeks. Keep track of any additional errors the proofreaders begin seeing, so the errors can be incorporated into the training next time.

And yes, there should be a next time. Like time on the firearms range, writing training needs to be repeated. Add new things, rearrange, say it in different ways, but writing clarity needs to be addressed at least annually, even if the program is simply a 30-minute exercise attached to a staff meeting.

Your approach is even more important in writing than it is in other types of instruction. In training and when correcting errors, always remember the rule I gave you in the opening. Writing is personal. We create it. It comes from us, like our children. Criticizing our writing is like saying we have an ugly baby.

If you believe an on-site writing class specifically designed for probation staff by a retired probation officer would be a useful addition at any point in the process, or if you would like additional copies of this manual, please contact my colleagues or me through the Favoritetrainers.com website, at its email address, administrator@favoritetrainers.com.

Getting someone to attend a writing class or read a writing manual is a tough sell. Thank you for your interest, thank you for your dedication to your profession, and thank you for allowing me to still be associated with it.

Danny R. Kuhn

REFERENCES

(A note on editions and availability: There may be newer editions of these venerable reference manuals than those referenced here, but the manuals seem to change little from year to year in the areas we use most. The *Gregg* and *Chicago* are quite hefty and expensive when bought new. Used copies can often be found on Amazon.com for a whopping 1¢ plus the obligatory postage and shipping. If you think they strongly resemble the code and guideline books we use every day, you are not alone.)

Gregg Reference Manual: A Manual of Style, Grammar, Usage, and Formatting by William A. Sabin. Richard D. Irwin, Inc., 11th edition (2011)

The Chicago Manual of Style. University of Chicago Press, 16th edition (2010)

The Elements of Style, Fourth Edition, by William Strunk Jr. and E. B. White. Pearson, 4th edition (1999)

The petit and eloquent *Elements of Style* was used in college writing classes throughout the Baby Boom and Gen X generations, so there may be an old one somewhere in your attic. Dr. William Strunk Jr. was a brilliant English professor at Cornell. He compiled his simple rules in a little book for use in his own classroom. In 1919, one of his students was smitten by its beauty and usefulness.

That student was E. B. White, who went on to write *Charlotte's Web, Stuart Little, The Trumpet of the Swan,* and many other beloved works. Macmillan, the original publisher, asked him to revise Strunk's work (the professor had gone on to that great musty classroom in the sky by that time) for the college and popular markets in 1957.

Talk about a hit! The California Book Company's store on the campus of UC Berkley sent the following telegram to Macmillan on August 20, 1959:

We confirm order PO-3595 for 200 Strunk Elements of Style College Edition STOP In addition send 300 more college edition STOP Whole campus gone wild STOP

Imagine that. UC Berkley, whole campus gone wild over *The Elements of Style.* What a difference the next decade would make in the "campus gone wild" category.

BROUGHT TO YOU BY:

Danny Kuhn is a graduate of Marshall and West Virginia Universities and is a former high school science teacher. He also had a 20-year career as a United States probation officer, and was deputy chief for the Southern District of West Virginia when he retired in 2010. Since then, he has continued conducting court training programs around the country on topics such as writing, team building, communication, and performance. He is the author of historical fiction novels *Fezziwig: A Life* and *Thoreau's Wound* (Knox Robinson Publishing, London and Atlanta) as well as several nonfiction works. He lives in Myrtle Beach, South Carolina, and can be reached through the website www.favoritetrainers.com.

Hilarie Gaylin (M.Ed., The George Washington University, B.A., Bryn Mawr College) is a former senior instructional designer/trainer for the United States Senate Office of Education and Training in

Washington, DC; training specialist for the United States Capitol Visitor Center; and director of education and training for the United States District Court, Eastern District of Virginia. She designs and delivers customized workshops and provides consulting and coaching services, as described on her website www.hilariegaylin.com.

Seth Ellison is a graduate of the Savannah College of Art and Design (B.F.A., Fine and Studio Arts) and The University of the Arts, Philadelphia (M.F.A., Fine and Studio Arts). He is a web content editor for Educational Testing Service in Princeton, New Jersey.

Additional copies of this book are available via the world's largest online retail site, or by contacting administrator@favoritetrainers.com, a DUNS registered provider of government services.

Made in the USA
Monee, IL
04 November 2026

67381719R10095